21
Easy Steps To
Financial Security

Alvin H. Danenberg, D.D.S., C.F.P.

International Publishing Corporation
Chicago, Illinois

Library of Congress number: 95-75150

ISBN: 0-942641-66-3

This publication is designed to provide accurate information in regard to the subject matter covered. It is sold with the understanding that the authors and publisher are not engaged in rendering legal, accounting, or other professional services. If legal advice or other expert assistance is required, the services of a competent professional person should be sought. (From a declaration of principles jointly adopted by a committee of the American Bar Association and a committee of publishers.)

Table of Contents

Introduction: Let's Get Serious

If you are serious about making a difference in your financial future, you must act now. You can't just say that you have decided to make a difference in your financial future. You must actually do it. Consider the following analogy:

Three frogs sat on a lily pad. One decided to jump off. How many frogs were left?

You may think the obvious answer is two. Actually, the answer is three. You see, although one frog *decided* to jump off, he only *decided* to jump. He didn't actually do it. He thought about it; he *decided* to do it; but he didn't follow through.

How many times have you decided to start your diet, but never did? How many times have you promised yourself to quit smoking, but never did? How many times have you vowed to begin a regular exercise program, but never did?

In our hectic lives, we *decide* to do many things, but we only act on a few. You must do more than just *decide*. You must jump off your indecision pad and make it happen now.

My guess is that each of you would like to achieve complete financial security at some point in time. If this were not true, you would not have chosen to read this book. You are already ahead of the game. Just think, you've only read 232 words, and you are into the journey.

My definition of financial security is: *that point in time when you can live the lifestyle you have chosen, financed from the assets you have accumulated, without the need of any additional income.*

Yet, surveys show that the majority of us don't know how to get there. Like the pieces of a puzzle, you may have some knowledge about money and investing, but you don't quite understand how to put it all together. Even though the challenge to reach this goal may appear to be beyond your abilities, it's not! So, let's get serious and try to put this puzzle together.

A 2,000 piece jigsaw puzzle is much more difficult to put together than a 21½ piece puzzle. Reaching financial security does not have to be a 2,000 piece challenge. Conceptually, it can be reduced to just a few critical pieces. In that way, the process becomes simpler and more understandable; the end result more achievable. This book identifies the 21½ easy steps to put together the financial security puzzle.

You may want to think of them as action steps. Some may be of higher priority to you. However, they all are important. If you understand each step completely, then the puzzle comes together more easily.

At the beginning of each step, there is a listing of the highlighted points you will learn after mastering that step. There are also many sample worksheets that are already filled out to be used as examples as well as blank worksheets for you to use personally. Take your time, and review these action steps as often as you find it necessary.

We'll start by my introducing you to a 30-year-old, married couple, Jodi and Mike, and their 5-year-old daughter, Jane. They will provide the real-life examples referred to throughout this book. They are both employed with a combined gross income of $47,320. They are motivated and have taken up the challenge of receiving financial direction. You will follow them as they create their own path to financial security using 21½ easy steps.

Find a comfortable chair, put your feet up, and let's get started.

1

Know Where You Are Financially

You will learn how to . . .

- *fill out your own Personal Financial Statement*
- *fill out your own Cash Flow Statement*
- *find where you are financially as you start*

When you begin a board game like *Monopoly*™ or *Life*™, you put your playing piece on *Start*; you get a specific amount of play money and game pieces; and you're off! In other words, you are given a predetermined starting point financially.

In real life, the game is a journey; and one objective is to reach financial security.

Let's start with today. You most likely already own some things. However, you need to have a tally of what you actually own—where you are financially—so that you can build from there.

To do this you need to prepare two statements—a Personal Financial Statement and a Cash Flow Statement. I'm going to describe these statements and provide samples for review and blank forms for you to use. In Step 15, I'll refer back to these statements so that you can project your retirement needs into the future.

Personal Financial Statement

A *Personal Financial Statement* is your statement of how much you are worth in dollars after you add up all of your assets and then subtract out all of your debts. Your assets can be divided into three categories—cash or cash equivalents, investments, and use-assets. See Figures 1-1 and 1-2.

Cash or *cash equivalents* are liquid assets which can be used as cash. For example, money in a savings account or a money market fund. *Investments* are generally not as liquid as those in the first category. They may actually be very illiquid. Examples include stocks, bonds, CDs, retirement accounts, real estate, business ownership assets, and limited partnerships. *Use-assets* are material things you own and use that have a value but you do not intend to sell. These include your home, cars, boats, jewelry, clothing, and other personal property.

Your *debts* include everything you owe to the banks, friends, credit card companies, mortgage companies, etc.

To prepare your statement, add up the value of all your assets by taking an inventory. Then, determine what it will cost to pay off all your debts today. If necessary, you can contact your creditors (banks, credit card and mortgage companies, etc.) to get the pay-off balances as of a certain date. Subtract your debts from your assets, and the result will be your current *net worth*—your *bottom line* financial position today. You will want to prepare your Personal Financial Statement at least annually to help you see how you are progressing as you increase your net worth.

Cash Flow Statement

A *Cash Flow Statement* shows all your sources of income for the year, and how they are spent. See Figures 1-3 and 1-4. This analysis will reveal your pattern of spending, saving, and investing. Your inflow of cash will include gross salaries and wages, interest and dividend income, rental income, etc. Your outflow will be divided into savings and investments, fixed expenses, and variable expenses. Fixed expenses such as mortgage and note payments, insurance payments, taxes, etc. are predictable and recurring. Variable expenses are those you have some degree of control over such as expenses for food, clothing, entertainment, utilities, etc. If you pay everything by check, you will have a record to help you reconstruct what you spent in each category.

The outcome of the Cash Flow Statement is that you will learn where your money is actually going. You may learn that you are spending too much in certain categories at the expense of other important

Figure 1-1: Mike and Jodi's Personal Financial Statement

Mike and Jodi's statement of financial position as of December 31, 1994

ASSETS[1]

Cash/Cash Equivalents

Checking account	$3,050
Credit union savings account	4,000
Money market account	3,500

Total Cash/Cash Equiv. | **$10,550**

Invested Assets

Stock portfolio	$4,300
CDs	5,000
IRAs[2]	1,000

LIABILITIES AND NET WORTH

Liabilities[3]

Credit card balance	$950
Auto note balance	4,920
Mortgage note balance	81,900

TOTAL LIABILITIES | **$87,770**

Total Invested Assets	$10,300

Use Assets

Residence	$105,000
Automobiles	14,000
Personal property	20,000

Total Use Assets	$139,000

TOTAL ASSETS	**$159,850**

NET WORTH   **$72,080**

1. Presented at fair market value
2. Mike, $500; Jodi, $500
3. Principal only (pay-off balances)

Figure 1-2: Your Personal Financial Statement

For:

Date:

ASSETS[1]

Cash/Cash Equivalents

Total Cash/Cash Equiv.

Invested Assets

LIABILITIES AND NET WORTH

Liabilities[2]

TOTAL LIABILITIES

NET WORTH

Total Invested Assets

Use Assets

Total Use Assets

TOTAL ASSETS

1. Presented at fair market value
2. Principal only (pay-off balances)

Figure 1-3: Mike and Jodi's Cash Flow Statement

Mike and Jodi's cash flow statement as of December 31, 1994

INFLOWS

Gross salaries	$47,320
Dividend income	572
Interest income	225
Savings[1]	3,000
TOTAL INFLOWS	**$51,117**

OUTFLOWS

Savings and Investments[2]   **$1,800**

Fixed Outflows

Taxes[3]	$11,291
Mortgage note payments[4]	8,750
Debt payments[5]	2,880
Insurance premiums[6]	2,340
Total Fixed Outflows	**25,261**

Variable Outflows	
Food (includes dining out)	$8,050
Transportation, gas, auto maintenance	3,125
Clothing/personal care	3,295
Entertainment/vacations	3,186
Medical/dental care	1,600
Utilities/household expenses	4,300
Miscellaneous	500
Total Variable Outflows	24,056

TOTAL OUTFLOWS $51,117

1. Withdrawal from credit union savings account
2. $1,000 IRA contribution and $800 deposit to money market account
3. FICA, Federal, and state income taxes
4. Includes principal, interest, insurance, and property taxes
5. All debt (principal and interest) other than mortgage
6. Automobile and life insurance premiums (health paid by employers)

Figure 1-4: Cash Flow Statement

For:
Date:

INFLOWS

TOTAL INFLOWS

OUTFLOWS
I. Savings and Investments

Fixed Outflows

II. **Total Fixed Outflows**

Variable Outflows

III. **Total Variable Outflows**

TOTAL OUTFLOWS

ones. You could then realign your spending habits by budgeting yourself to spend less in one category and more in another.

For example, you may be spending too much on entertainment and not enough on savings. You may want to put an additional $100 a month into savings and reduce your entertainment spending $100.

It is critical that part of your cash flow goes into a savings or investment vehicle. If it is not at this point, don't worry about it. Once you have completed this book, you *will* be saving for your future.

2

Set Goals

You will learn . . .

- *the importance of setting and writing down goals*
- *how to write short-, intermediate-, and long-term goals*

You must set goals. Without goals, it's like building a house without a blueprint; it's like steering a ship without a rudder. Without goals, you keep trudging along with no direction. You flounder. Ernest Hemingway succinctly said, "Never confuse motion with action."

A study at a major university evaluated different individuals over a period of years and their commitment to goal setting. The results were amazing. Researchers discovered that only 3% of all the people tested actually set goals and wrote them down on paper; 10% had specific goals and tried to work toward them but never committed them to paper; 60% had vague goals like, "I want to be rich" or "I want to be successful." The last 27% didn't know the difference between a wish and a goal. These individuals basically lived a day at a time with no concept of the future.

By themselves, these facts were enlightening. However, the following statistics were mind boggling. The study went on to identify that the 3% who actually had goals and wrote them down had basically similar backgrounds and variables as did the next 10% of the individuals who had solid goals but did not write them down. Yet, the 3% who actually took the time to write down their goals, who actually committed their specific desires to paper, were 10% to over 100% wealthier than the next 10% who did not make the additional effort to write down their goals. What a revelation!

The reason probably lies in the fact that you think more about your goals when you write them down and refer back to them frequently. They're on your mind. You consciously and subconsciously direct your actions toward the achievement of those important goals.

Be in the top 3%! Write down your goals, and update them at least every six months! Be specific! Write down exactly *what* you want, *when* you want to achieve it, and *how* you will go about getting it. Napoleon Hill claimed, "Anything the mind can believe and conceive, it can achieve."

Look at the *Goals Sheet* (see Figure 2-1) and start the process. Decide what you want to accomplish in different areas of your life six months, one-, five- and ten-years from now. It's OK to change your mind It's even OK not to know exactly what you want at this point.

Flexibility is important because changes and adjustments are healthy and necessary. Therefore, review your Goals Sheet every six months.

Look at Jodi and Mike's Goal Sheet (Figure 2-2). They have thought out their short-, intermediate-, and long-term goals.

For each specific goal, write down how and when you will attain that goal. Look at the *When and How Sheet*. Again, be prepared to make changes along the way. Here is one of Mikes' specific goals (see Figure 2-3).

At this point, you probably don't know the specific details of how you will attain financial security or when that might occur. However, as you progress through this book, and you formulate your plan of attack, the details will come. Then, you will be able to fill out your *When and How* Sheets with ease (Figure 2-4).

Figure 2-1: Jodi and Mike's Goals

	Personal/Family	Financial	Business
6 Months	spend more time with family in evening make repairs around house	complete financial statement and cash flow statement set up budget establish emergency fund review all insurance begin retirement plan	ask for raise write marketing plan for new business
1 Year	take vacation to Disney World with family purchase second car build deck onto house	begin college education fund eliminate as much short-term debt as possible plan retirement in 25 years get financial papers in order	start own business

5 Years	*plan for 2 one-week vacations a year* *remodel kitchen*	*be debt-free except for home mortgage* *plan for retirement in 20 years*	*expand business to gross sales of $1 million*
10 Years	*purchase vacation home* *buy RV or boat*	*begin looking for retirement property* *plan retirement in 15 years*	*expand business to gross sales of $2 million*

Figure 2-2: Your Goals Worksheet

	Personal/Family	Financial	Business
6 Months			
1 Year			

5 Years

10 Years

Figure 2-3: Mike's When & How Worksheet

Mike

GOAL   *start my own restaurant*

WHEN?   *I will have my new restaurant open by January 1, 1997*

HOW?

I will do the research necessary and have my marketing plan completed in 3 months. My financial papers will be ready for the bank within 6 months. I will have all the necessary construction plans completed within 9 months. I will have the restaurant open for business within 1 year.

_____   _____
signature   date

Figure 2-4: Your When & How Worksheet

GOAL   _____

WHEN?   _____

HOW?

_____ signature

_____ date

3

Live Beneath Your Means

You will learn . . .

- *enough is enough*
- *how to develop your Needs List*

The only way you can accumulate the money necessary to insure financial security is to spend less than you earn. It's that simple. You need excess cash to create financial security. If you spend everything you earn, there will be nothing left over; spend more than you earn, then you can really get into trouble.

By spending less than you earn, you have the necessary cash to invest and save for your financial security. In the following Steps you will learn the specific methods to make this money work best for you.

There is only so much that you need in order to merely survive. Above that, there are certain comforts you want. And finally above that, there are luxuries you would like to have to pamper and indulge yourself. These desires for comfort and luxuries are good and healthy. But, only to a limit—enough is enough.

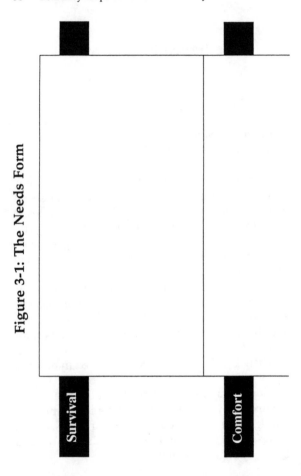

Figure 3-1: The Needs Form

Luxury

Figure 3-2: Jodi and Mike's Needs List

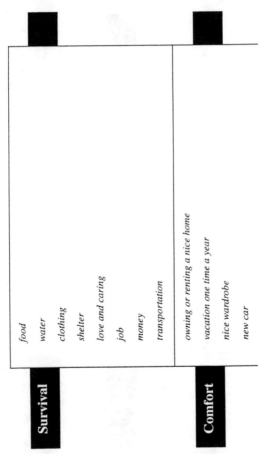

Survival

food
water
clothing
shelter
love and caring
job
money
transportation

Comfort

owning or renting a nice home
vacation one time a year
nice wardrobe
new car

Luxury

dining out

stereo

TV

golf or tennis lessons

VCR

vacation home

trip to foreign country

expensive jewelry

two automobiles

domestic help

boat

designer clothing

join a country club

You need to take the time to think about which survival, comfort, and luxury items you need and want. Take some time to daydream. Come up with some specific survival, comfort, and luxury items that fit your personality. Use the *Needs Form* on the preceding pages (Figure 3-1) to organize your thoughts. Here are some ideas Jodi and Mike considered (see Figure 3-2).

Examples of survival items include food, basic clothing, and shelter. Comfort items would include dining out, fashionable clothes, and a dream house. Luxuries might include a live-in cook, expensive jewelry, and a luxurious vacation home. You need to make the decisions for yourself. But, remember, enough is enough! Avoid being greedy.

If you are fearful of your financial future, you may feel insecure. This feeling may lead you to feel the need to have more material possessions. This is not necessarily greed. It is a manifestation of your financial insecurity. Once you realize that you are on your way to a financially secure future, then these manifestations of insecurities will disappear. Your perceived *need* for material things will diminish.

I'm suggesting that you *should* have wants and desires. And goal setting is the way to plan for them. You must live beneath your means to accomplish the security you desire. This book will teach you to become financially secure—not greedy!

4

Develop an Emergency Fund

You will learn . . .

- *why you must have an emergency fund*
- *how to set up an emergency fund*

Several years ago, Jodi and Mike went through some bad times. Mike lost his job, and they had no real savings on which to fall back. Although Jodi had a full time job, her income was not sufficient to maintain their standard of living. It took about five months before Mike was able to get back to work, doing what he wanted to do, and earning what he needed to earn. Those five months were extremely difficult times for the family. If Jodi and Mike had only saved for such a situation, they would have not suffered as they did. They were stressed both financially and emotionally.

Your initial savings goal should be to develop an emergency fund which should equal three to six months of your living expenses. You have already determined your living expenses in Step 1 in your Cash Flow Statement. It's summarized there for easy access.

For example, Jodi and Mike's annual living expenses are $49,317 (Fixed Outflow + Variable Outflow).

Dividing this by 4 gives their three months' living expenses ($12,329.25); dividing by 2 gives their six months' living expenses ($24,658.50). Therefore, Jodi and Mike should accumulate between $12,000 and $25,000 in their emergency fund.

Should anything happen to cut off your cash flow, this emergency money (your security blanket) would be available to keep you financially viable.

Obviously this money must be in a safe and in an easily accessible account such as in a government money market fund which offers check writing privileges. Although government money market funds are not guaranteed, they are backed by the full faith and credit of the United States Government. Almost all mutual fund companies as well as discount brokerage firms offer such funds. More detail about this in Steps 12 and 16. But, if you want to establish an account right away, call one of the discount brokers listed in Step 16. Tell them you want to open a government money market account with check writing privileges. Later, you will use the same discount broker to establish separate investment accounts which I discuss later. Dealing with only one discount brokerage firm is convenient and simple.

Use the emergency account only for its intended purpose—an emergency. Examples may include: to pay the deductible on an insurance policy, to pay for emergency home or car repairs, or to pay unexpected taxes. Needless to say, if you were out of work for an extended period of time, the dollars would be available.

Keep in mind, whenever money is removed from the emergency account, it must be replaced as soon as possible. This is a critical account!

This account must be separate from all other investment accounts and should be identified for what it actually is.

For example, Mike and Jodi renamed their "money market account" (which contained $3,500) "Jodi and Mike's Family Emergency Fund" so there would be no question what this account was destined to do. The cash in their credit union savings account ($4,000) was transferred to this fund bringing it to a total of $7,500. When their CDs come due, they will transfer that $5,000 into the emergency fund for a grand total of $12,500. This is certainly adequate for their immediate needs. Depending on how much of a safety net Jodi and Mike desire, they can leave the emergency fund as is, or they can add to it until it reaches $25,000.

It is important that this emergency fund not be a part of another savings account. If a portion of a savings account is earmarked for an emergency, somehow the commingled money always seems to be used for other purposes. Remember, this money is set aside as a source for ready cash in times of need. Don't invade it unless you must.

5

Use Insurance Wisely

You will learn . . .

- *when to use insurance*
- *which risks to cover by insurance*

Risk management is a financial planning tool to shift the risk of catastrophic financial loss to a third party—namely an insurance company. For a fee (the premium), the insurance company bets you won't have a loss, and you bet that you will. If you do suffer a loss, then the insurance company takes over the financial responsibility based on the provisions of the policy.

A catastrophic loss would be financially painful for you to absorb. Losses you can afford should not be covered by insurance. Cover them out-of-pocket or with your emergency fund.

When evaluating your specific situation, consider all areas of your life which may require insurance coverage. Protection should be an entire package, not a *hit and miss* deal and should include insurance for life, health, disability, business overhead, personal and professional property loss, personal and professional liability, and business interruption.

Shop around for the best prices and be sure you are comparing *apples* to *apples*. What may appear to be an inexpensive policy may not cover what you really need. Insurance experts say the biggest reason consumers pay for more than they need is because they simply don't bother to explore the options.

Also keep in mind that the cost of a policy can be reduced if a higher deductible (e.g., health insurance) or a longer waiting period (e.g., disability insurance) is assumed before the insurance kicks in.

Contact a professional who knows insurance and can be objective. A fee-for-service Certified Financial Planner™ can review your current exposure to potential losses and can recommend proper methods for protection.

You can also get useful information from the National Insurance Consumer Help Line by calling (800) 942-4242. This is a service of the Insurance Information Institute in New York, and the Health Insurance Association of America and the American Counsel of Life Insurance both in Washington, DC.

The following descriptions should help you evaluate your own needs:

Life Insurance

Life insurance does not benefit you; it benefits others. It replaces the loss of income from you to others because of premature death. It basically can provide liquidity to your family, to your business, and to partners.

Life insurance is designed to be used as a risk avoidance method. This means the risk of financial disaster that would fall on your family or business partners if you were to die prematurely, is transferred to the insurance company. The company will pay your beneficiaries the face value of the policy. The insurance company accepts this risk because of the quarterly, semiannual, or annual premiums paid over the years. In summary, for a price, your obligations are met after your death.

All life insurance is based on the chance of you dying at a specific age and is the basis that determines what insurance companies will charge you. To this base, their profit is added and called the premium. This is known as term life insurance.

Cash value life insurance is term insurance combined with a type of savings plan or investment. This type of insurance is packaged under different names such as whole life insurance, universal life insurance, and variable life insurance. Usually, sales commissions are attached to this investment package as well as profits for the insurance company. Cash value life insurance is not what pure life insurance is all about.

Many life insurance policies currently in force are superfluous or inefficient. Among the unnecessary are small or overpriced term insurance policies, whole life policies which only accrue cash values at 3% or 4%, mortgage life and credit life insurance sold by lenders, insurance on children, and funeral insurance. Consider eliminating or replacing these types of policies if they are part of your insurance package because costs outweigh the benefits.

As an informed consumer, you are better off in the long run if you buy term insurance to replace the future cash flow needs of your beneficiaries. If you have a cash value policy, you may want to replace it with a term life policy and invest the difference. As you will see, there are much better and more efficient ways of creating wealth than through cash value life insurance contracts.

Insurance Information Inc. is a service to help you find the least expensive life policies available for your situation. This is a fee-for-service company which does the research independently for you. (They do not sell insurance, nor do they receive a commission from the insurance companies. You must go to the individual insurance companies and make your purchase.) You can reach them at (800) 472-5800.

Also, don't forget your professional organizations. Often they have negotiated very low rates with life insurance companies for excellent term coverage.

Health Insurance

The government may change the entire complexion of health coverage. But, for the present, each of us must protect ourselves against the potential costs of major medical expenses. Remember, insurance should only cover catastrophic financial losses.

You may also need to plan for long-term-care insurance (which covers nursing care in and out of institutions). After you become eligible for Medicare insurance, you need to plan for *Medigap* insurance (which covers what Medicare does not cover).

Disability Insurance

Statistically, you are much more likely to suffer a disability during your working years than you are to die prematurely. Consider those policies which cover your occupation and the way you physically work within that occupation.

For example, if you are a dentist with an active clinical practice, you want a policy that will provide benefits to you if you couldn't physically practice clinical dentistry any longer even though you could still physically instruct students in a dental school.

Business Overhead Insurance

Associated with disability insurance is business overhead insurance. If you own a business and become disabled, business overhead insurance should cover your daily business expenses and pay your employees. Business overhead insurance is specialized to cover these expenses if you are unable to work.

Property Insurance

If your home burns down to the ground, or your new automobile is totally destroyed, you would have a significant financial loss without proper insurance. Property insurance protects you against such losses due to specific causes (or perils).

For example, fire, theft, rain, hail, and wind damage are usually included in a standard homeowner's policy. However, some perils are not included and must be added as separate riders such as earthquake and flood coverage. If you have a loss that was due to flooding, but you did not have flood insurance, then your loss would not be covered at all!

When purchasing homeowner's insurance, be sure your coverage is for *replacement value*. You don't want a policy that only covers the *market value* today.

For instance, a house's *replacement value* is far more than its *market value*, especially if it's older and has special features. The same goes for personal belongings. The *market value* of an old couch may be $11.95, but replacing it may cost 300 times that amount. Be safe, and only purchase insurance that will replace a loss at the value it costs to replace it today.

Liability Insurance

You are responsible if someone is injured on your property or is harmed by your actions or inactions. To protect you from financial loss due to these occurrences, you need personal liability insurance and professional liability insurance.

Personal liability insurance is usually part of property insurance coverage such as homeowner's and automobile policies. Coverage above policy limits is provided through the additional purchase of an umbrella insurance policy.

For example, automobile insurance is usually a package of *liability* and *damage to your automobile* with varying maximum dollar limits of coverage. The *liability* portion is for *bodily injury per person*, *bodily injury per accident*, and *property damage other than to your car per accident*. *Damage to your automobile* is separated between *collision damage* and *other than collision damage*.

Professional liability insurance is usually written as a separate policy by companies specializing in that area. Each profession has its unique characteristics which must be evaluated.

Business Interruption Insurance

If your business cannot function because of storm damage, power failure, fire, etc., your daily expenses (rent, salaries, etc.) still go on. Business interruption insurance helps cover these expenses by providing a stated daily benefit to you. With this type of insurance, you must also include riders for earthquake and flood.

Also, it is important to understand the difference between *on-premises-perils* and *off-premises-perils*. You need to be covered for both if you own a business!

As an example, if there is a major power failure in your community which occurs completely off your property but results in loss of power to your office for one week, your office cannot operate. If your business interruption insurance only covers *on-premises-perils*, then you will not be covered for the loss of one week's income. On the other hand, if your policy covered *off-premises-perils* in addition to *on-premises-perils*, you would be covered for that lost week.

My personal experience with business interruption insurance relates to the destruction from Hurricane Hugo in Charleston, SC in 1989. Some dental offices in Charleston did not have flood insurance to cover rising water from the storm surge. Also, many offices did not have *off-premises-perils* to cover the loss of electric power for over a month in some areas. This is a lesson worth learning!

•

A potential roadblock to hinder your journey to financial security is to have a catastrophic financial loss. Many potential risks can be protected by insurance. Use insurance wisely to help keep you on track.

Not all insurance companies are the same. You should check on the soundness of the insurance companies you are investigating. Most libraries have copies of three of the most reliable sources for these statistics: A. M. Best & Co., Moody's Investors Services, and Standard & Poor's (S&P) Insurance Rating Services. You can also get specific company information for a fee by calling Weiss Research at (800) 289-9222.

As your life cycle changes, your insurance needs will also change. It is important to monitor your changing exposure to risk annually. In this way, you, your insurance agent, and your financial advisor can adjust your coverage appropriately.

Let me emphasize that the bottom line is to use risk management to protect yourself from catastrophic financial losses. Insurance is not intended to cover all losses. Deductibles are used to reduce the premiums you must pay since you will assume a specific degree of loss.

You should consider those policies with the highest deductible you can afford. The higher the deductible, the lower the premium. However, there is a point above which higher deductibles do not reduce the premium proportionately. Be sure to investigate.

An ideal planning tool would be for you to purchase a high deductible policy. Then, take the savings in premiums between the low deductible policy and the higher deductible policy, and invest that savings in a no-load growth mutual fund. When it comes time to pay any required deductible, your invested savings should have grown significantly over time to more than cover the out-of-pocket expenses.

I will discuss investments later. Keep reading to get the whole picture. Remember, there are only 21½ pieces to the puzzle, and already you are assembling the fifth piece.

6

Understand and Use Compounding

You will learn . . .

- *the power of compounding*
- *the common denominator to all investments*

Ignorance of how money works is inexcusable in a capitalistic, entrepreneurial society such as ours. Why isn't money taught in our schools? The history and function of money are taught but not the essence of money. Money is what we receive in exchange for our goods and services. It represents a value for what we have provided. It can then be used to purchase additional goods and services. This has been the function of money throughout history.

Up to this point, most people are quite familiar and comfortable with the workings of money. However, money can also create money. This is where many people get lost. Everyone needs to understand how money can make money through the incredible power of compounding.

Compounding was called the eighth wonder of the world by Albert Einstein. *Compounding,* the process of interest being added back to principal to continue to earn more interest, can make the smallest sums of money grow into significant fortunes. Try to picture the following allegory:

In 1492, Christopher Columbus decided he was going to save for retirement. He had one penny ($0.01), and he knew he could earn 6% every year on his money. He put the penny in his left pocket and placed the interest ($0.01 x 6% = $0.0006) into his right pocket for safekeeping. He never added anything to his original penny in his left pocket. Yet, the interest accumulated year after year in his right pocket.

Chris was a very healthy guy: He lived until today, 1995—503 years later—and decided to retire. So, he took his one penny from his left pocket and added it to the simple interest in his right pocket. Do you know how much Mr. Columbus had?

Well, the interest in his right pocket added up to only $0.30 (503 years x $0.0006 = $0.30). Along with his original penny from his left pocket, he had $0.31 on which to retire. Not good planning!

What could Chris have done differently? Let's assume Chris was much more astute about investing because he knew about compounding. Instead of putting the interest in his right pocket, he put it into his left pocket with the original penny—the principal. Over the years he would earn the same 6% interest on the original penny and the accumulated interest in his left pocket.

As the story goes, at the end of year #1, he had $0.0106 in his left pocket (the original penny plus the 6% interest). At the end of year #2, he had $0.011236 ($0.0106 plus 6% interest). At the end of year #3, he had $0.01191 ($0.011236 plus 6% interest). This is called compounding and continued for Chris for 503 years. How much did good ol' Chris finally accumulate for retirement?

The answer is somewhat more to Chris's liking. At the end of 503 years of compounding the original penny at 6% interest, Chris had $53,561,191,327 (53 billion, 561 million, 191 thousand, 327 dollars!) That's a lot of pocket change!

This story emphasizes the phenomenal and exponential power of compounding. None of you will live 503 years. But, all of you will have more than just one penny to invest and will have the ability to compound your investments at higher rates of return.

Now, consider the following example.

If you place $2,000 annually into one of several excellent mutual funds which compounds yearly at 15%, at the end of five years you would have invested $10,000, but it would have grown to $15,507. At the end of ten years you would have invested $20,000, but it would have grown to $46,699. At the end of thirty years you would have invested $60,000, but it would have grown to $999,914. The longer you allow compounding to work its miracle, the more impressive the results. Look at Table 6-1 below to see just how effective compounding is in creating significant wealth. (I will discuss mutual funds in Steps 12 and 16).

When you think of investing, think of the end result. Think of what the average compounded total return is. If you compare one investment to another, always compare their average compounded returns. This is the common denominator among different investments. It helps place the comparison on a *level playing field*.

As a piece of the puzzle, compounding becomes an important catalyst in your quest to reach financial security. When used properly in an investment program, its power to create wealth becomes extraordinary.

You're on a roll. Don't stop now! On to Step 7!

Table 6-1: Compound Table

$2,000 contribution beginning each year
15% compounding each year

You will have . . .

After these years	Actually invested	Accumulated wealth
5	$10,000	$15,507
10	$20,000	$46,699
15	$30,000	$109,435
20	$40,000	$235,620
25	$50,000	$489,424
30	$60,000	$999,914
35	$70,000	$2,026,691

7

Avoid Unnecessary Debt

You will learn . . .

- *the dangers of debt*
- *how much debt is unhealthy*
- *how to get out of debt*

Debt can destroy wealth and your ability to create wealth. It's easy to get into debt today. The advertising industry has led us to believe that anything you want is there for the asking—just pay later. After you realize the burden your debt repayments have placed on your budget, you may then experience a feeling of foreboding which can further prevent you from taking the proper steps to reach your financial security. Some financial geniuses have allowed their debt to become so overbearing that their wealth dissipated into bankruptcy.

Debt is not terrible. You must know the trade-offs, and keep them in balance. Ideally, your debt should equal no more than 20% of all your assets. That's your goal. When debt rises to over 40% of all your assets, you could get into trouble.

Debt also is more expensive to repay. Here's what it cost Jodi and Mike to take a $10,000 personal loan.

Jodi and Mike took a personal loan for $10,000 at 18% interest to be repaid in equal monthly payments of $293.75 over four years. The total repayment will equal $10,000 plus $4,100 in interest. In order to repay $14,100, Jodi and Mike must earn enough income to first pay their federal and state income taxes and then their loan and interest charges. In this oversimplified example, they will need to earn $20,043 in order to pay: 1. the $5,943 in federal taxes, at 15%, social security and medicare taxes at 7.65%, and state taxes at 7%, 2. the $10,000 in principal borrowed, and 3. the $4,100 in interest accrued. It will cost Jodi and Mike $10,043 above what they borrowed to repay their original $10,000 loan.

If you took out such a loan, and your tax bracket were higher, then your total cost to repay that loan would also be much higher. Debt can get very expensive.

Look at your Personal Financial Statement and Cash Flow Statement completed in Step 1. You will see how much you are spending on debt repayment. If you find yourself in a debt crisis, you should stop spending except for the absolute necessities. Don't panic. Think this through. You will be amazed to find out what you really don't need.

Determine which of your debts has the highest interest rate and pay this debt first. Sometimes consolidating many smaller debts which have high interest rates into a larger loan with a lower interest rate can be very helpful. Get out of your unnecessary debt, and get on with your financial puzzle.

You may not realize it, but your personal history of credit and debt is on file and is available to anyone who legitimately wants to *check you out*. You have the right to review this information and to challenge any inaccuracies. You should contact one of the following compilers of credit information at least once a year. For a fee, you can obtain a copy of your most recent credit report: TRW (800) 392-1122, Trans Union (800) 851-2674, and Equifax (800) 685-1111.

8

Buy a Home Only If . . .

You will learn . . .

- *about the emotional side of buying a home*
- *about the economic side of buying a home*
- *how to determine if you should buy or rent*

There are emotional and economic reasons for purchasing a home. Frequently, the emotional reasons far outweigh the economic advantages. That's OK! But, make sure you know the differences.

Pride of ownership and sentimental feelings mean a great deal to many people. If you want to own your home because you feel good knowing it's yours, then purchase your home. (Of course, you must be able to afford it. A good rule of thumb is that your monthly mortgage payments of principal and interest should not be more than one-fourth of your monthly gross income minus other long-term debt expenses.) You can fix it up, enlarge it, and care for it as you wish. Sentimental reasons may tie you to a home you've inherited or lived in for most of your life. These reasons may make the economic advantages and disadvantages moot.

Some economic realities will make owning your own home very profitable; some will make you just break even with renting; some will cost you plenty. Following are some general areas for you to consider to determine how your home stacks up as an investment.

- Up-front down payment to the mortgage company
- Buyer's closing costs
- Monthly principal and interest payments
- Monthly taxes and insurance
- Average annual maintenance expenses
- Seller's closing costs
- Commission to a real estate agent when selling a home

Purchasing a home is like long-term investing. You pay a specific sum of money up-front and then you continue to feed that investment over time. Some of the money you put into this investment can add to the value of your home, some can be deducted from your taxes, and some becomes expenses that you cannot recoup.

Your down payment is the out-of-pocket amount of money your mortgage company requires. Closing costs are also paid up-front. Your down payment will only be working for you to the extent that the value of your home is appreciating; closing costs do not add to the value. Some may reduce your taxes over time, but they are essentially lost expenses.

As you reduce the monthly principal of your mortgage, you are feeding money into your investment. It's adding to your ownership (known as equity) in your home. The interest you pay monthly does not reduce principal; therefore, it does not go toward the equity. It is, however, a tax deductible expense.

Along with your monthly principal and interest payments, you are also paying real estate taxes and homeowner's insurance. Your mortgage company takes the monthly amount you pay toward these expenses and keeps it in an escrow account and draws on them when they are due. Taxes can be deducted on your tax return, not the cost of insurance.

Routine maintenance expenses do not add to the value of your home and are not reimbursed when you sell. Structural changes, such as adding on a room, will add some value when you sell. The cost of these structural changes are added to the original cost of your home by increasing your *cost basis*.

When you sell your home, you will have seller's closing costs to pay. This comes off the total amount of money you receive for the sale of your home, thus reducing your actual profit. Another selling expense will be for the real estate agent's commission which may be as high as 6% to 8% of the selling price.

The bottom line is that you will put up a specific amount of money to get into your home; you will have various expenses along the way; and you will have additional costs to sell your home. Considering the appreciation of your home and then subtracting out all of the expenses, you will have a net profit (or possibly a net loss). How does that profit compare to the profit or loss you would realize if you otherwise invested the difference between the projected costs of renting and those of owning?

Here is a detailed comparison of the projected costs and profit potential of ownership and those of renting similar properties which Jodi and Mike now face. The purpose in presenting this example which has many variables and assumptions is to make you think about the alternatives. Your particular situation must take into account the actual numbers that exist in your part of the country.

- The original value of both residencies is $105,000.
- The purchased home appreciates at 4% a year.
- The rental home's lease increases at 4% a year.
- The real estate taxes, homeowner's insurance, and renter's insurance stay level over 15 years.
- A 15 year mortgage can be secured at the fixed rate of 9%.

- The mortgage company requires a down payment of 20%.
- A no-load mutual fund which has a history of compounding at 15% a year is available.
- The rental home has an annual rental rate of approximately 7% of the value of the purchased home.
- Renter's insurance is approximately one-third the cost of homeowner's insurance.
- Real estate taxes are approximately 1% annually for the purchased home.
- The marginal tax bracket is 22% (Federal 15%, State 7%).
- Real estate commission is 6%.
- Repairs and maintenance average $1,000 a year for the homeowner.
- No structural improvements are made to the purchased home.

Mike and Jodi purchased their $105,000 home with a $21,000 down payment. The equity in their home will grow as the home appreciates. Their total annual payments to their mortgage company equals $12,124. At the end of 15 years, their house has appreciated to $189,099, but they have paid out-of-pocket $21,000 for the initial down payment, $181,860 to their mortgage company, and $15,000 in repairs and maintenance. Because of their tax bracket and their ability to deduct a percentage of their real estate taxes and mortgage *interest, they saved $18,813 in taxes over 15 years. When they go to sell their home, they have to pay a 6% real estate commission which is deducted from the gross sales price. The bottom line over 15 years is that it costs Mike and Jodi $21,294 to live in their home (an investment loss of $21,294).*

As renters, Mike and Jodi could have invested the $21,000 down payment into a no-load mutual fund averaging 15% compounded return a year. They also could have invested annually what they saved between total renter's expenses and total owner's expenses. They could have paid the taxes due on their invest-ment gains out of the mutual fund every year. At the end of 15 years, their mutual fund would have been worth $216,680. Their total costs to rent over 15 years would have equaled $160,684. Mike and Jodi could have realized a profit of $55,996.

The critical decision which makes *this* rental scenario more attractive financially is that the initial money which would have provided a down pay-ment for ownership is invested instead. And, the annual savings from not having homeowner's payments and expenses are also invested. See Figures 8-1 and 8-2.

Are you surprised? As you can see from the bottom line in each example, Mike and Jodi would make a wise investment choice to rent a home and invest the difference rather than to purchase a comparable home. However, your situation will be different. Take the time to determine your numbers and have your accountant help you with the details and actual computations.

Where do you stand when it comes to the investment potential of owning your own home? Should you rent instead and invest the difference? Does it make sense to you both emotionally and economically? Remember, the end result of assembling all 21½ puzzle pieces is to reach financial security. Which option leads you in the right direction?

Figure 8-1: Jodi and Mike's Home Ownership Example

Home value = $105,000

Down payment (20% of value) = $21,000

Finance $84,000 at 9% over 15 years

Interest and principal = $10,224 a year

Real estate taxes = $1,077 a year

Homeowner's insurance = $823 a year

Total payment to mortgage company = $12,124 a year

Total payment to mortgage company over 15
   years = $181,860

Total interest over 15 years = $69,360

Total real estate taxes over 15 years = $16,155

Income taxes saved from interest paid over 15 years = $15,259

Income taxes saved from real estate taxes paid over 15 years = $3,554

Appreciated home value after 15 years = $189,099

Profit (loss) over 15 years

   $189,099 appreciated value

       + $15,259 income tax saved from mortgage interest

       + $3,554 income tax saved from real estate taxes

       - $21,000 down payment

       - $181,860 total paid to mortgage company

       - $11,346 6% real estate commission on sale of home

       - $15,000 maintenance and repairs

   ($21,294) loss

Figure 8-2: Jodi and Mike's Home Rental Example

Home value = $105,000

Invested

    (20% of value) = $21,000 in mutual fund

    Annual savings between owner's costs and renter's costs added to fund each year

    15% average compounded return adjusted for taxes due = 11.7%

    Total value of mutual fund after 15 years and all income taxes paid = $216,680

Rent over 15 years

    Lease = $650 a month with annual increases of 4%

    Renter's insurance = $300 a year

    Total rent over 15 years = $156,184

    Total renter's insurance over 15 years = $4,500

    Total payment in rent and insurance over 15 years = $160,684

Profit (loss) over 15 years

    $216,680 value of mutual fund after taxes paid annually

        - $156,184 total paid to landlord

        - $4,500 total paid for renter's insurance

    $55,996 profit

9

Make the Tax Laws Work for You

You will learn . . .

- *what tax avoidance means*
- *what tax-deferral means*
- *how tax-deferral and compounding creates wealth*
- *what types of retirement plans are available*

The tax laws are complex, and they are constantly changing. Don't worry! I'm not going to bore you with them, nor am I going to suggest that you study them. You can leave the details to a tax attorney and/or an accountant.

However, there are some basics that you should know. The tax laws that work to your advantage can be divided into two general areas: Tax Avoidance and Tax Deferral.

Tax avoidance allows you to reduce the amount of taxes you pay the government. *Tax deferral* allows you to postpone paying some of your taxes until retirement. Both methods are important to understand because they will allow you to keep more of your money for investment and growth.

Tax Avoidance Methods

Tax avoidance methods are *write-offs* against your income. They reduce your taxes because they lower your taxable income. In special situations, your actual tax liability can also be reduced through tax credits.

Some of the *write-offs* that can reduce your income include contributions to your Individual Retirement Account (IRA), personal exemptions, business expenses, medical and dental expenses, other taxes you have paid (such as real estate taxes, state income taxes, and personal property taxes), interest you have paid on your home mortgage, donations to charities, investment losses, and casualty and theft losses.

How much these *write-offs* will reduce your income tax depends on your income level and the actual amount of the deductions. If you use an accountant, he or she can and should advise you regarding any deductions you are entitled to.

It is your right to reduce your taxes to the maximum extent allowed by law. Don't settle for less.

Make sure your accountant or tax preparer is working *for* you. If he or she does not discuss deductions and their potential benefits, then you might need to consider finding a more knowledge-able tax professional.

Any money you save by reducing your taxes should be considered a bonus. Take this new found money and invest it as I will describe in Steps 12 and 15. You will thank me profusely many years from now. I will graciously accept your gratitude prematurely and say, "You're welcome!"

Tax Deferral Methods

Tax-deferral methods allow you to postpone some taxes until retirement. With many tax-deferred plans, the IRS allows you to deduct your annual contribution to your tax-deferred plan when you file your tax return. This reduces your income tax for that year. The money that accumulates in your tax-deferred account will grow without taxes being levied until you retire and/or withdraw it. All of the interest, dividends, and capital gains earned in your tax-deferred account can be reinvested without being taxed. Remember the story about Christopher Columbus in Step 6 and the power of compounding? Your money will be working hard for you.

Here is an example explaining the difference between investing in a tax-deferred account and a taxable account:

Let's assume you and your spouse both have earned income and you plan to invest a total of $4,000 at the beginning of each year into your Individual Retirement Accounts (IRAs). If you wanted to retire in 25 years, you and your spouse would have invested a total of $100,000 over the course of 25 years.

You have decided to invest in a no-load mutual fund that appreciates on average at 15% a year. (Step 16 lists several mutual funds that have a history of 15% or greater over the last 10 years.) At the end of 25 years, you will have accumulated approximately $979,000! If your combined federal and state tax bracket were 28% then, and these taxes were paid as you withdrew this amount over a period of years from your retirement plans, then the $979,000 would have an after-tax value of approximately $704,880.

Now assume the same scenario except you invest the money in a taxable rather than a tax-deferred investment account. You will have to pay taxes every year on the $4,000 invested and on the accumulated interest, dividends, and capital gains. In this case, at the end of 25 years, only $354,163 will have accumulated.

With a tax-deferred plan, you will have approximately *$350,000 more* for retirement because you utilized the gift the U.S. Government gave you—the tax-deferred provision in the U.S. tax code.

There are three types of tax-deferred vehicles which you should consider: Individual Retirement Accounts (IRAs), Qualified Retirement Plans, and Variable Annuities.

Individual Retirement Account (IRA)

If you have earned income during a calendar year, you can set up an IRA even if you participate in another retirement plan. In the year you reach age 70½, you cannot. You can establish an IRA with several types of organizations: banks and similar savings institutions, mutual funds, stock brokerage firms, and insurance companies. The simplicity of setting up an account (Step 16) will amaze you.

You can contribute up to $2,000 or 100% of your earned income, whichever is less, each year. These contributions will be fully deductible from your current income for the year you make the contributions unless you also participate in an employer's qualified retirement plan. Then, some or all of your IRA contributions may not be deductible.

You can begin withdrawing money from your IRA without penalty after you reach age 59½. You must start withdrawing money by April 1 of the year following the year you reach age 70½. (There is also a way you can begin retirement before age 59½—explained in Step 21.)

There are penalties that could result if you fail to follow certain rules. These include:

• Excess contribution—contributing too much to your IRA

• Early withdrawal—taking money out of your IRA prior to age 59½

• Excess distribution—taking too much money out of your IRA once you reach age 59½

• Excess accumulation—not taking money out of your IRA after you reach age 70½

• Prohibited transaction—using your IRA in a way that is not allowed

• Failing to file Form 8606 for nondeductible contributions or overstating nondeductible contributions

An IRA can also be set up for a spouse (Spousal IRA) who does not receive any compensation for the year in question. This must be a separate account—not a joint one. However, a joint tax return must be filed for the year a Spousal IRA is set up. The total combined contributions you can make each year to your IRA and a Spousal IRA is the smaller of $2,250 or your earned income for the year. This can be divided between your IRA and the Spousal IRA in any way you choose.

You can have as many IRAs as you wish. However, during any single year, your total contributions cannot exceed the lesser of $2,000 (or $2,250 with a Spousal IRA) or 100% of your earned income.

You can set up an IRA and contribute to it for a particular year as late as April 15 of the following year. For example, for the taxable year of 1995, you can contribute to an IRA as late as April 15, 1996.

As I stated earlier, if you or your spouse are covered by an employer's retirement plan at anytime during the year, your allowable deduction may be reduced or eliminated depending on the amount of your income and your tax filing status. Be sure to check with your accountant or tax preparer for all the specifics. Remember, even if you cannot *write-off* any IRA contributions, you can still benefit greatly from having a tax-deferred account.

Qualified Retirement Plans

Qualified plans are retirement plans that are approved by the IRS and must meet three requirements. They:

1. must be for the exclusive benefit of employees or their beneficiaries,

2. must be given to the participants in a written document, and

3. cannot discriminate in favor of officers, stockholders, or highly paid employees.

These plans must also comply with minimum eligibility, vesting, and funding requirements. Of the eight plans available, each has its advantages, disadvantages, and contribution limits. My favorite,

the Simplified Employee Pension (SEP), is unbeliev-
ably simple to implement if you are in business for
yourself—with or without employees. The remaining seven are various qualified plans that are
provided by employers to their employees and
require more complex documentation and professional advice to administer.

I will first discuss all eight in general terms. Then
I will be more specific about my favorite—the SEP.

1. **Profit Sharing Plan:** This is one of the most
common qualified retirement plans. The employer
makes contributions for the employees as a percentage of their salaries.

2. **SEP:** The Simplified Employee Pension works
like a Profit Sharing Plan when it comes to contributions. These contributions are made by the owner
of a business to each of the employee's IRAs as
well as to the owner's own IRA. (These are set up
as separate SEP-IRA accounts.)

3. **401(k) Plan:** This is a very popular plan with
employees since they determine how much of their
own pay is to be contributed to the plan. Sometimes there is a "matching employer contribution."

4. **SARSEP:** The Salary Reduction Simplified
Employee Pension is a mixture of the SEP and the
401(k) Plan. Each employee elects how much of
their salary they will contribute to their IRA.

5. **Age Weighted Profit Sharing Plan:** This plan
offers the benefits of a Profit Sharing Plan but per-

mits a larger portion of the contributions to be allocated to the accounts of older employees.

6. **Money Purchase Pension Plan:** A specific annual contribution by the employer to the plan is mandatory. As a trade-off, employees can contribute a higher percentage of their salary.

7. **Target Benefit Plan:** This plan functions like the Age Weighted Profit Sharing Plan, but annual contributions are mandatory.

8. **Defined Benefit Plan:** This plan requires mandatory contributions that are higher for older employees. The main advantage of this plan is that annual contributions are not limited to a specific percentage of salary or to a specific dollar amount.

Now, back to my favorite, the Simplified Employee Pension (SEP). A SEP is a written plan that allows employers to make contributions toward their own, as well as employees', retirement accounts. Contributions are made to each participant's IRA (set up as a SEP-IRA). All qualified employees *must* have their own SEP-IRAs. A qualified employee is the employer as well as any employee who is at least 21 years old, has worked for the employer at least 3 of the 5 years immediately preceding the tax year, and has received from the employer at least $385 in compensation in the tax year.

A very simple two-sided form, (Form 5305-SEP), is all that needs to be filled out and distributed to employees. It couldn't be any easier!

You may not be familiar with this type of retirement plan. It seems to be a well-kept secret. But, it is powerful. There are no tax attorneys needed to draw up the document, and there are no annual filings with the IRS. The government has really made this one simple and inexpensive.

The SEP rules permit the employer to contribute each year to each employee's SEP-IRA up to 15% of the employee's compensation or $22,500, whichever is less.

For self-employed individuals, the compensation is the net earnings from self-employment. In this case, net earnings must take into account the deduction for contributions to a SEP-IRA. The IRS provides a formula to determine the exact amount that can be contributed to a SEP-IRA. However, it works out to a maximum percentage of approximately 13.04% of your net earnings—not 15%.

If you are an employee, your employer's contributions on your behalf are not included in your wages on your Form W-2. These contributions are excluded from your income.

Variable Annuities

Variable annuities are contracts with life insurance companies in which you can invest for retirement. You decide how to allocate your money among several professionally managed portfolios of stocks, bonds, and cash equivalent vehicles which are similar to mutual funds. You can switch between these portfolios as you see fit. There are no guarantees of safety of principal or rate of return. At retirement, you will have several distribution options from which to choose. If you withdraw money from the annuity before age 59½, there are penalties imposed by the IRS as well as the annuity company. (Again, Step 21 will explain how you can retire before 59½ with no penalties.)

Only consider variable annuities after you have invested the maximum possible into your IRA and any other qualified retirement plans available to you. There is no maximum limit to the amount you can invest in a variable annuity, and, if you're self-employed, you do not have to make any contributions for employees. But, the money you put into a variable annuity is not tax-deductible as it is in an IRA or a qualified retirement account. However, the accumulated amount is tax-deferred. Also, annuities charge fees above those of mutual funds, and those fees are deducted from your portfolio value annually.

You will need to investigate the many variable annuities to determine those with the lowest expenses as well as the best managed portfolios for your needs. (Variable annuities are packaged with insurance contracts. Be sure you know what you are purchasing.) A service that can help you locate a good annuity is Independent Advantage Financial and Insurance Services, Inc. (800-829-2887). They do not charge you a fee, but they do receive a commission from the annuity company. One low-expense variable annuity with a good selection of managed portfolios is *The Best Of America IV* annuity offered by Nationwide Life Insurance Company (800-848-6331).

The following free information may be helpful to you and is available from the IRS at 800-829-3676. Request publications: 590, Individual Retirement Arrangements; 560, Retirement Plans for the Self-employed; and 571, Pension and Annuity Income. Also request forms: 5305-SEP, Simplified Employee Pension–Individual Retirement Accounts Contribution Agreement; 5305A-SEP, Salary Reduction and Other Elective Employee Pension–Individual Retirement Accounts Contribution Agreement; 8606, Nondeductible IRAs; and 5498 Individual Retirement Arrangement Information.

I have tried to reduce Step 9 to the essential information you need to know. I hope I have not put you to sleep. If I did, wake up!

The money you are saving in taxes and then investing either in a taxable or tax-deferred account is going to make you *big bucks*. Whatever you do, don't drop out now. This is the ninth piece of the puzzle. You're almost halfway there! Let's continue.

10

Prepare Basic Estate Planning Documents

You will learn . . .

- *the importance of a will*
- *the importance of a living will*
- *the importance of a durable power of attorney*
- *how to organize all of your important papers*

This Step is short and will introduce you to three very important documents: the *will*, the *living will*, and the *durable power of attorney*. All three documents fall under state law which means you will need to contact an attorney in your home state to advise you. My purpose is to describe the salient features of each.

No one wants to talk about death and incapacity, but it still needs to be addressed. If for no other reason, you want to know that your loved ones won't have to be burdened with a myriad of paperwork, attorneys, and problems that could have been avoided by planning ahead. These three documents will assist the natural process of passing on to your heirs the financial security you are creating now.

The Will

Everyone is going to die eventually. When that happens, everything you own or have control over must pass on to someone else. A *will* is nothing more than a legal document that specifies what goes to whom after your death. State laws govern how your personal property will be transferred *if* you do not have a will.

Everything you own with someone else as a *joint tenant with right of survivorship* goes to that person no matter what the *will* or State law says. After your death, your *will* is entered into probate where the *will* is presented to a court and an executor is appointed to carry out its instructions. It is nothing more complicated than that.

Of course, how assets are allocated can get more detailed depending on the complexity of your estate. However, the bottom line is that a *will* lets it be known to everyone how you want to have your estate dispersed after your death. The alternative, to let the state laws dictate how to divide up your property, is totally ridiculous.

Therefore, I suggest you contact your attorney and have your *will* drawn up as soon as possible if you have not already done so. Also, as circumstances and laws change, you will need to update your *will*. Changes in your life such as marriage, divorce, and children require you to at least review your will and then have it amended properly.

The Living Will

This is another legal document that clearly states your wishes. In this document, you are letting everyone know what you want your physicians to do if it should become necessary to put you on artificial life support.

This is an emotional question to answer. Give it serious thought. Discuss it with your spouse and family as well as with your physician, attorney, and clergyman.

In a *living will* you state your desire to be kept alive by artificial means or to allow your physicians to let you die naturally.

If this document does not exist, then the stress and anguish that your loved ones will be under in such a medical emergency will be more difficult for them to handle. Take the time now to save your family additional emotional trauma if such a situation should ever arise.

The Durable Power of Attorney

It is possible that you could sustain a medical problem that would leave you mentally incapable of handling your legal and personal business. You could be alive but mentally unable to function. A *durable power of attorney* is a document that states that if you should be declared mentally incapacitated, then a designated individual or individuals whom you have already appointed will be legally able to execute the specific legal functions you identify on your behalf.

If a durable power of attorney did not exist, then your family would have to go to court to obtain the proper legal authority to handle your affairs. This would be time consuming, expensive, and extremely traumatic for your loved ones.

Again, this is a simple document for your attorney to prepare. But, it is something that takes considerable thought on your part—you would be giving control of almost everything you own to another individual. First, make sure that this individual is *the* right person. Second, make sure that this individual wants to have such control and responsibility. The person whom you grant a durable power of attorney will need to spend time on your behalf if you should become incapacitated.

The person to whom you grant this *power* does not have to be given the power right away. You could design it so that the power becomes effective only *after* you are declared to be incapacitated. This is referred to as a *Springing Durable Power of Attorney*.

The three documents I have just described should be prepared by your attorney. To expedite matters, they can all be done at one time. The overriding factor in having these documents in place is to reduce the emotional and physical stress that will fall on your loved ones if these documents did not exist. You and your spouse will need separate documents.

Copies of these documents should be given to your attorney, accountant, and others of responsibility. The originals should be stored in a safe place such as a safe deposit box. Along with these documents there should also be a list of where other important documents and papers can be found. For example, this list might include the following items and their locations:

- Prior tax returns
- Insurance papers
- Stock, bond, and other investment information
- Real estate papers
- Accounts payable and receivable
- Inventory of personal use-assets
- Inventory of collectibles such as (stamps, coins, etc.)
- Business papers (partnership, corporate, documents, etc.)
- Phone numbers of attorney, accountant, and other professionals involved with your assets

- Account numbers and locations of various savings, checking, and money market accounts

Preparing this information in an organized fashion will eliminate many hours of searching and frustration for those trying to put together the facts about your assets. For more specific information and worksheets on getting organized, you may want to purchase *The Beneficiary Book* for approximately $30. It is also available on IBM disk.

The Beneficiary Book is a three ring binder with the following chapters: Personal Questions, Final Arrangements, Your Estate, Your Finances, Your Investments, Personal Possessions, Your Business, and Closing Thoughts. The purpose of the book is to provide a simple, logical method of centralizing important information pertaining to your life. Call 800-222-9125 for more information.

11

Consider the Benefits of Trusts

You will learn . . .

- *what trusts are*
- *how trusts may be helpful*
- *various types of trusts to investigate*

The use of trusts dates back to medieval England. Back then *necessity* proved to be the *mother of invention*. The *necessity* began when kings in days of old would often overtax and overregulate real estate to the chagrin of many land owners. The *invention* was created by wise attorneys to get around these burdensome laws. And so, trusts were born.

Title to land was given by the original owner to persons he could trust. The trustees (the persons who managed the property) administered the land for the original owner. After the original owner's death, the trustee disposed of the property according to the original owner's wishes.

Today, trusts have evolved into highly sophisticated tools for the convenient management of one's assets.

It used to be that only the very wealthy knew about and benefited from trusts. However, trusts are available today to anyone who wishes to benefit from them.

Why should you be interested in trusts? Because, you can arrange to educate your children through trusts. You can take care of your elderly parents through trusts. You can avoid probate through trusts. You can protect assets from creditors through trusts. You can even create a retirement income for yourself and your spouse through trusts.

Basically, a trust enables you to create a financial plan that meets your needs as well as the needs of your loved ones. It helps guarantee the future.

Trusts are legal matters and tend to get technical and downright boring. I'll try to elevate the rest of this discussion so it is several notches above being complicated and dull. But, bear with me for awhile first. Here comes the legal stuff:

By definition, a trust is a legal arrangement which can hold the ownership of assets for the benefit of one or more individuals (beneficiaries). You (the grantor) can establish the trust to fulfill your wishes. You can be the manager of the trust (the trustee) or you can name someone else to be the trustee. The trust files annual tax returns and pays taxes on retained income. This last statement is important for you to realize. The federal income taxes due on taxable retained income above $7,500 is 39.6%!

A trust can be set up that takes effect now (a living trust) or after your death (a testamentary trust). If it takes effect now, it can be either a revocable trust (one whose terms you can change at anytime) or an irrevocable trust (one whose terms you can never change). Most irrevocable trusts are designed to protect assets from creditors. All testamentary trusts are irrevocable.

Are you still with me? You may want to reread the above paragraphs until you are completely familiar with the terminology. OK! Let's continue!

Typical assets which can be placed in a trust include bank accounts, real estate, securities, mutual fund shares, limited partnerships, and personal property such as art, cars, and jewelry. All assets that become part of the trust must have the ownership transferred to that of the trust. For example, if you placed your car into a trust, the car could no longer be in your name and the title would read, "In trust for . . . *the beneficiary's name.*" If you have a safe deposit box, also change ownership to that of the trust. Remember, your assets cannot be included in the trust until legal title has been changed.

There are many types of trusts for many varied purposes. An attorney who specializes in them can advise you regarding how trusts may be able to assist you in reaching and maintaining your financial security. Since trusts are governed by state law, the attorney should be from your home state.

A Sample of Trusts

Following are a few you may want to know about.

Revocable Living Trust

A living trust can eliminate the cost and publicity of probate, making the transfer of assets after death uncomplicated. Be aware, however, this type of trust does not reduce estate taxes and does not protect assets from creditors.

Credit Trust or Bypass Trust

This is a testamentary trust (takes effect after death) which allows your estate to save estate taxes on up to $600,000 of your estate's value. This is in addition to the $600,000 of assets a surviving spouse is able to leave tax-free in the estate.

2503(c) Trust

This irrevocable trust is sometimes called an education trust or age 21 trust and can be used for college education expenses. Each year, you and your spouse can jointly contribute up to $20,000 to this trust free of gift taxes. The interest earned can grow within this trust for future use. However, the trust must terminate when the child reaches 21 years of age unless the child agrees to an extension.

The trustee has the expressed right to distribute income to the child for his or her support, care, maintenance, and education. However, trust assets cannot be used to pay for the *necessities of life*. (Check with your attorney to determine how your state defines *necessities of life*.)

As with most irrevocable trusts, assets in the trust can be protected from creditors by including specific wording.

Charitable Remainder Trust

This is an irrevocable living trust. It can save substantial amounts of federal estate and income taxes as well as create retirement income. It will allow you to transfer an appreciated asset to the trust. In exchange, the trust will pay you and your spouse an income for life. The remaining assets in the trust will then go to the charity you have designated. This is an ideal retirement planning vehicle.

Here is an example of how a charitable remainder trust can work for Jodi and Mike. (Remember them?):

Let's assume Jodi and Mike have received a gift of an undeveloped piece of property which has appreciated in value several times its original cost but does not generate any income. If they were to sell the property, they would have a large tax bite because of the substantial capital gain. If they gave that property to their children to get it out of their estate, they would have gift taxes to pay on the transfer. If they just kept the property, they would not enjoy any cash flow presently, and their estate would then be responsible for the federal estate taxes after their death.

Now, let's assume that Jodi and Mike transfer this piece of property to a charitable remainder trust, and the trust in turn sells the property for $150,000. The trust then invests the proceeds and pays Jodi and Mike $9,000 (6% of the sale price of the property) each year for the rest of their lives.

Here's what happens. The trust does not have to pay any capital gains tax because it is owned by a charitable organization which is tax-exempt. Jodi and Mike will receive $9,000 each year for life from the asset which yielded $0 prior to the transaction. Although Jodi and Mike will have to pay income tax on the $9,000, they will also get a charitable contribution deduction on their personal federal income tax return because of their donation. This deduction will be equal to the value of what is expected to be left over for the charity after they die. This value is determined from an IRS actuarial table based on their age and the an-

nual percent return they receive from the trust. In addition, Jodi and Mike do not have to pay any gift taxes when they set up the trust since it is a charitable donation. Finally, none of the assets which remain in the trust will be taxed to their estate or the trust's estate because the assets are owned by a charity.

Well, I've made it, and I hope you did too! This has been a brief introduction to the fascinating but legal world of trusts. Your attorney and tax advisor can guide and advise you regarding the pros and cons of trusts for your specific needs.

Wealth Transfer Planning, Inc. is another source you may want to contact for additional information. You can speak with Charles Douglas, JD, CFP or Cory Grant, JD at 800-423-4890. Seek out their advice. It may prove to be a very important piece to your financial puzzle.

Are you finally ready to start investing to make some money? Step 12 begins to open up the door to investing opportunities *according to Danenberg*. These are my ideas and my philosophy. They work for me. They should work for you.

12

Educate Yourself About Investing

You will learn . . .

- *why you should invest in the stock market*
- *why mutual funds are the answer*
- *when the U.S. stock market is on sale*
- *when the U.S. stock market is overpriced*

Investing is defined as using capital to create more money. It connotes the idea that the safety of your investment dollars is most important. This is in contrast to *speculation* which implies far more risk or *gambling* which is the extreme of speculation.

My philosophy is based on investing in ways that make good sense to me utilizing investment vehicles I understand. I want to be able to control my investments; I want to be able to take out my cash when I want it; and I want to be comfortable with the historical performance of the investment. If my philosophy and yours are in sync, then the rest of this book will be *just what the dentist ordered.*

Over the years, many investment vehicles and their long-term results have been investigated—housing, U.S. farmland, stocks, bonds, certificates of deposit, gold, silver, diamonds, oil, old masters' paintings, stamps, foreign currencies, Chinese ceramics, etc. The U.S. stock market has consistently ranked among the best of all investment vehicles over the long-term for total returns. In addition, the stock market is easy to follow, understand, and liquidate (to sell for cash quickly). And, to make life easier, there is a specific vehicle within the stock market that leaves the professional responsibility of management and stock selection in the hands of those who do it for a living. I am referring to mutual funds.

As I take you through this step, first I'm going to go into detail about mutual funds. Then, I'm going to suggest a way for you to determine how expensive (overvalued) or inexpensive (undervalued) the overall stock market is based on over one hundred years of stock market history.

This powerful tool will put you well above the average investor. Yes, this is going to be a very exciting and useful way for you to become a successful stock market investor. Actually, it will even put you well above a large percentage of professional money managers.

Mutual Funds

Mutual funds are pools made up of money coming from you and me and many other investors. The fund manager then takes this money and invests it by purchasing various stocks and other securities for the portfolio. All expenses for the management of the fund are paid out of the total assets in this portfolio. The price of each share of the fund is equal to the value of the assets in the portfolio after all expenses have been paid divided by the number of shares outstanding.

For example, if the portfolio value minus expenses on a specific day is $50,000,000 and there are 2,000,000 shares outstanding, the price of one share is $50,000,000 ÷ 2,000,000 or $25 per share. This is called the net asset value (NAV).

At the end of every trading day, the fund reports its net asset value which is also reported in almost all financial sections of daily newspapers across the country. If you wanted to buy or sell one share of a fund, the NAV is the value of that share for that specific day. Remember, this price changes daily.

Follow me as I take you deeper into the world of mutual funds. I will not allow you to wander off and get lost. That's my promise! Watch your footing! Here we go!

There are two broad categories of mutual funds: load and no-load. There are approximately 4,000 load funds and 600 no-load funds.

Load funds have a sales commission added to the NAV of the fund which is a commission for brokers and agents who sell the funds. For every load fund

there is usually a comparable no-load fund available. (There is also a category called *low-load* which
refers to those funds which charge less that 3%
commissions.)

No-load funds are the funds I invest in. They are
sold directly by the fund company, and no sales
commissions are added to the NAV. Why pay the
commission for load funds?

If you need advice from a sales agent, then the
sales agent deserves to be paid a commission for
his or her advice. In Step 16 I'll show you how to
do your homework so you will not need the advice
of a sales agent. Therefore, you will never need to
pay commissions since you will only be purchasing
no-load funds.

Categories of Mutual Funds

Within all mutual funds, there are various categories or types of funds. The funds which make up
each category invest the pool of portfolio money
based on specific objectives. The objectives identify
the types of investments the fund will invest in
(such as U.S. stocks, bonds, foreign securities,
precious metals, options, etc.) as well as how
aggressive or conservative its investment techniques
will be (such as borrowing money, purchasing
options, hedging, etc.). The following categories

help to summarize what is available to the mutual fund investor.

Aggressive Growth Funds

The investment objective of this category is maximum capital gains. These funds invest primarily in stocks with significant growth potential as well as high risk. They may also use leverage by borrowing money to purchase securities and by trading in stock options and index futures. Also, many of these funds may concentrate their investing in specific industries or segments of the market. They may do very well in bull markets (when prices are moving up) but may do very poorly in bear markets (when prices are moving down). These funds are specifically suited for the long-term investor (at least five years) who is not looking for current income or dividends.

Growth Funds

These funds are similar to the aggressive group except they usually do not engage in leveraging—they do not borrow money to purchase securities nor do they trade in stock options and index futures. They generally invest in growth oriented companies that are more mature and pay some cash dividends. They are also better diversified than the aggressive funds. As a rule, growth funds will move in the same direction as the general stock market in both bull and bear cycles.

Growth & Income Funds

These funds will invest in securities of well-established companies that pay high cash dividends. Income is an important objective along with long-term growth. These funds may be more stable than the general market.

Balanced Funds

Within these funds, a large portion of the portfolio is devoted to stocks and bonds between which the fund manager can move assets based on the conditions of the marketplace. There is significant overlap between this category and that of Growth & Income. These funds provide a high dividend yield and are more stable than the general market.

Bond Funds

As the name implies, these funds only invest in fixed-income securities—bonds. These are further subdivided into corporate, government, mortgage-backed, general, and tax-exempt bond funds. The date when bonds come due (maturity date) determines the risk of the fund. Short-term bonds coming due within three years have much less risk and are therefore more stable than long-term bonds coming due more than ten years. Bond funds offer very little growth potential.

International Bond Funds

These fixed-income securities are from foreign companies and governments. There is more risk involved than with U.S. bond funds because of currency rate fluctuations and foreign government stability.

International Stock Funds

These funds invest in stocks of foreign companies. As with the international bond funds, there is added risk beyond U.S. stock funds because of government stability and currency fluctuations.

Sector Funds

These funds are industry specific. There are funds investing only in health related companies, utilities, financial institutions, communications, etc. These funds may respond independently from the general market.

Precious Metals Funds

Generally, these are classified as sector funds. However, precious metals funds are the most volatile and therefore the most risky of all mutual funds and deserve a separate category. These funds invest in mining stocks as well as bullion.

Index Funds

These funds invest in the stocks that make up specific market indices such as the S&P 500 Index, the Over-the-Counter Index, etc. Their purpose is to mimic the up and down trends of the indices they represent. They usually have lower management fees.

Money Market Funds

Money market funds invest in short-term money market instruments. These instruments are turned into cash usually within a few days. They consist of commercial paper, banker's acceptances, repurchase agreements, government securities, certificates of deposit, and other highly liquid and safe securities.

Money market funds act as a parking place for your money until it can be put to better use. That may mean that you eventually will spend it on the things you need and want, or you will invest it in other ways. The share value is held at a constant one dollar value per share. The percent return varies daily based on money market conditions. Most money market funds also provide check-writing privileges, which is a convenient way to instantly access your money.

There you have it. A summary of the categories of mutual funds. In Step 16, I will help you to create your plan and to choose those categories and the funds within those categories that meet your very own specific needs.

When the Market Is *On Sale;* When It Is Not!

I can't leave the subject of investing without discussing the best and the worst times to be invested in the U.S. stock market. The best time is when the market is *on sale* (undervalued); the worst time is when it is *overpriced* (overvalued).

If you were going to buy a piece of furniture for your home, and it was so popular that the store could not keep it in stock, the chances are that the price tag would be full retail. As a matter of fact, it might even be above retail because the store would

know that it could sell it for almost any price since
the demand was so great.

On the other hand, when that piece of furniture
had enjoyed all the buyers who wanted it, and the
store supply of that piece accumulated on the
showroom floor, the store would likely put it on
sale just to get rid of it. The store might eventually
sell the furniture piece for less than cost just to get
it out of inventory. At that point, the furniture
piece is still what you wanted, but it is now at a
rock-bottom price. When is the best time to buy the
furniture? Of course you're right! When the price is
at rock-bottom prices. And, that's also the best time
to buy the stock market—when it is at rock-bottom
prices (undervalued).

The price tag for the U.S. stock market has been
coined the Value Ratio by Walter Rouleau (Growth
Fund Research Inc., Box 6600, Rapid City, SD
57709). The Value Ratio is the Friday closing price
of the S&P 500 Index divided by the dividends
paid over the previous 52 weeks for the stocks
which make up the Index. The Value Ratio therefore is computed weekly.

Don't get nervous. I will describe all the details
about this ratio in Step 16. You will have no problem determining this ratio for yourself. It will take
all of one minute to figure it out. Remember, I
promised to walk you through this whole process

of investing with mutual funds. I will not let you down. Stick with me!

The importance of the ratio is that it has varied between 15 and 34 approximately 89% of the time since the 1870s! Before the creation of the S&P 500 Index in 1926, the Dow Jones Industrial Average was used to study this ratio.

Whenever the ratio is above 34 (5% of the time) or below 15 (6% of the time), the stock market is poised for a major change in trend. When above 34, the market eventually enters into a prolonged downtrend (or bear market); when below 15, the market eventually enters into a prolonged uptrend (or bull market).

The significance to the investor is that the U.S. stock market is overpriced (overvalued) when the Value Ratio is above 34 and is on sale (undervalued) when the Value Ratio is below 15. The essence of this ratio is that you, the investor, should become extremely cautious and conservative when the Value Ratio is above 34 and extremely aggressive when it is below 15.

I will describe my investment plan in Step 16 which takes advantage of this rare but extremely important *red tag special* known as the Value Ratio.

13

Know Your Investment Temperament

You will learn . . .

- *how to take your investment temperature*
- *which no-load mutual funds are right for you*

If you could take a thermometer and measure your *investment temperature*, what would it be? And, once you knew the reading, what would it mean?

I'm going to share a method with you which will help you determine your *investment temperature* which you will need to know before beginning any investment plan. Your *investment temperature* is actually a reading that identifies you as one of several investor-types based on your risk level. With this information, you can select the right investments to reach your ultimate financial goals.

Your *investment temperature* is not the same for all investment goals. For example, you may be a conservative-type for your child's college account; a growth-type for your retirement account; and yet an aggressive-type for your general investing account.

To determine your *investment temperature*, you need to determine your risk level for each investment goal you are considering. But, what is risk?

Risk is uncertainty. It's the up and down fluctuations in the stock market. For investors, it's the possibility that an investment may not perform well—maybe even lose principal. Your risk level is the degree of fluctuation that you personally can tolerate. It is the fine line between sleeping at night and insomnia.

If you were to accept too much risk, you might bail out of your investment at the wrong time. You might panic! John Templeton once said, "Don't panic. The time to sell is before the crash, not after."

One method which works is to examine the worst case scenario that you could accept over a 52 week period for each investment you are considering. In other words, how much downward fluctuation in your investment over a year's time could you accept before you could not sleep at night?

As an example, you have invested $10,000 toward a specific investment goal. Then consider the following downward fluctuations in value of your portfolio at the end of one year. The point at which you could not sleep at night is one level *beyond* your *investment temperature* for that investment. See Figure 13-1.

Your *investment temperature* labels you as a specific type of investor for the investment goal you are pursuing.

Let's get back to Jodi and Mike. They have determined they need to accumulate $100,000 for Jane's college education, and their investment temperature in this

Figure 13-1: Investment Thermometer

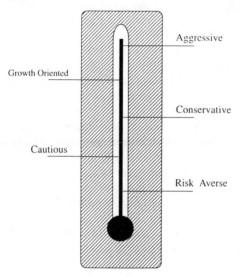

• Starting With A $10,000 Investment •

If you can accept a fluctuation   Then your *investment temperature*
over a one year period of...   for this investment goal is...

0% (no loss of principal) .... Risk averse

up to 5% drop (up to $500) .... Cautious

up to 15% drop (up to $1,500) .... Conservative

up to 25% drop (up to $2,500) .... Growth-Oriented

over 25% drop (over $2,500) .... Aggressive *case labels them as conservative investors. Their next step is to identify those categories of no-load mutual funds which fit this reading and their 13-year time horizon before they need the money.*

To find out which categories of funds are appropriate for Mike and Jodi, go to Table 13-1, the How To Choose Fund Categories table, and look under the Over 7 Years column. (You can also invest in any category less risky than your selected category. That means you can invest in any fund category appropriate for any time horizon shorter than yours and any temperature less risky.)

Jodi and Mike select their specific "investment temperature" which is "conservative." The categories of funds which fit their temperature are: Growth & Income and Long-Term Bond funds.

Here is an important comment about risk and time horizons: The longer you have to invest before you need your money, the less you need to consider risk as a critical factor. In other words, an investment program lasting ten years will smooth out almost all of the fluctuations of a volatile mutual fund.

A study reported in *Market Logic* newsletter (Issue #472, October 21, 1994) looked at the risk of owning all of the stocks in the New York Stock Exchange since 1871. During any one year period, the chance of incurring any loss was 30%. That's a great deal of risk! During any 5 year period of time, the chance of having any loss dropped to 11%. However, during any 10 year period of time, the chance of experiencing any loss was reduced to only 1%!

Although the metaphor of taking your investment temperature may seem a bit simplistic, it is an accurate way to view your investing temperament. Once you understand your risk level, choosing the best funds for your specific needs becomes an easier and more meaningful process.

You have assembled a major piece of your financial puzzle. You now know what type of investor you are and what types of no-load funds fit your temperament. Believe me when I tell you that most investors have no idea who they are or why they are investing the way they are. You are on the right track.

In Step 16, I will help you put your personal investing plan together integrating the concepts of the Value Ratio along with how to choose specific funds based on your investment temperature. Keep in mind that you and I are going through this together. Walk, do not run!

Table 13-1: How to Choose Fund Categories

Time Horizon

Investment Temperature	Up to 2 yrs.	2-4 yrs.	4-7 yrs.	Over 7 yrs.
Risk Averse	(Money market funds; actual purchase of U.S. Treasury securities* and zero-coupon bonds** for specific time horizon)			
Cautious	Money Market	Short-term Bond	Interm.-term Bond	Long-term Bond
Conservative	Money Market	Short-term Bond	Balanced / Interm.-term Bond	Growth & Income / Long-term Bond

	Money Market	Short-term Bond	Growth	Growth
Growth Oriented			International Stock International Bond	International Stock International Bond	Aggressive Growth Gold Stock Sector
Aggressive	Money Market	Short-term Bond	Aggressive Growth Gold Stock Sector	Aggressive Growth Gold Stock Sector

* U.S. Treasury securities: These are negotiable debt obligations of the U.S. government, secured by its full faith and credit and issued at various schedules and maturities. The income from Treasury securities is exempt from state and local, but not federal, taxes.

** Zero Coupon bonds: These bonds make no periodic interest payments. They are sold at a deep discount from its face value. The buyer of this bond receives the total accumulated rate of return when the bond is redeemed on a specific maturity date. For tax purposes, the IRS maintains that the holder of the zero coupon bond owes income tax on the interest that has accrued each year, even though the bond holder does not actually receive the cash until maturity.

14

Beware of Inflation

You will learn . . .

- *the hazards of inflation*
- *your break-even point*

The subtle but destructive nature of inflation can be dangerous to your financial health. Think of it as a hidden tax that keeps eroding or diluting the value of your money.

This book is not the forum to debate the political and economic forces that go into the creation of inflation. It is valid to state, however, that governments that print paper money have the ability to create inflation. And, the existence of inflation debases the value of a country's currency over time.

Consider this. The average inflation rate over the last 25 years has been 5.6% according to the U.S. Department of Labor. If inflation continues to average 5.6% over the next 25 years, then $1,000 in 1995 will only be worth $237 in purchasing power in the year 2020 (25 years from now)!

Neither you nor I can do very much to stop the inflationary cycle. But, you and I can protect ourselves financially by understanding its consequences, by realizing what it takes to offset its dilution effect, and by taking positive action to stay well ahead of it.

In order to offset the damage of inflation, you must obtain a total return from your investments that not only keeps up with inflation but also earns enough to pay the income tax due on the investment gain. Remember, investment returns are a taxable income source unless sheltered in a tax-deferred program.

How do you determine your break-even point? Here is a formula:

$$X = I \div (1- a)$$

X = required total return (%) on investment to break even with inflation

I = Inflation rate (%)

a = combined marginal tax bracket (in decimal form) for federal and state income taxes. (The marginal tax bracket is the income tax you must pay, expressed in decimals, on the next dollar you receive in income.)

For example, Jodi and Mike's taxable income for last year was $28,520, and their combined marginal tax bracket was 22%. The next dollar they would earn would be taxed at 22%. That means that for each additional dollar in income, $0.22 would go to taxes, and $0.78 would stay with them. If Mike and Jodi have a combined federal and state marginal income tax of 22% next year, and inflation is 5.6%, then their investment return next year must be 7.2% to just break even! Here is the calculation:

$$X = 5.6\% \div (1 - 0.22) =$$
$$5.6\% \div 0.78 =$$
$$7.2\%$$

At 7.2%, Jodi and Mike will only break even. They will not make any headway in their investing effort until they earn more than 7.2% in total returns.

Whether investing in a taxable or a tax-deferred environment, inflation is a factor to reckon with eventually. If you don't stay ahead of the game, you will fall behind. It is like rowing a boat in a river with the tide pushing you backward faster than you can row forward.

Check with your friends to see how many of them understand inflation and how many know what it does to future purchasing power. You'll be amazed about how much farther ahead you are in your journey to reach financial security.

15

Prepare for Retirement

You will learn . . .

- *how to project your needs into the future*
- *how to use a financial calculator*
- *how much you need to save for retirement*

Retirement may be a misnomer for many of us. A better phrase might be financial independence. Whatever you want to call it, I am referring to a point in time when you can live the lifestyle you have chosen, financed from the assets you have accumulated, without the need for any additional income. The question is, "How do you plan for it?"

In order for you to prepare and invest for retirement or financial independence, you need to have some idea of what your expenses will be. Just like any goal, you need to know what you are shooting for. Here's a way for you to start.

Refer to Step 1. You will be able to determine your present expenses from your Cash Flow Statement. That will be your starting point.

If you really knew what your future expenses would be, you could list them. However, most people don't know them. The next best thing is to take an educated guess. By using your current yearly expenses from your most recent Cash Flow Statement, you have a logical and practical point of reference. (If you haven't filled out your Cash Flow Statement yet, now would be a good time to do so.)

Some economists project that your expenses at retirement will be approximately 60% to 70% of what they are today (based on today's dollars). This is obviously a gross generalization. But, it is a basis to project into the future. Remember, all projections are just that. They can be revised or even totally discarded at any time.

Using the How Much Does It Take? worksheet and accompanying How Long Will It Last? table, you will be able to project how much money you will need in the future. This process will become simple, but at first it will be a challenge. Take your time to understand it.

Let's go through the four steps with Jodi and Mike.

1. Determine your current needs.

Use your present yearly expenses as identified from your Cash Flow Statement. You can add or subtract expenses that you know will or will not be included in the future. If you are not sure, you can use the 60% to 70% rule-of-thumb I mentioned. To be conservative, you can project 100% or even more!

The final dollar amount is what you think your yearly expenses at retirement will be (or whenever you want to reach financial independence) based on today's dollar.

Jodi and Mike have determined they will need 60% of their current total outflows or $30,670 a year in today's dollars when they retire.

2. Determine what these needs will cost in the future based on the dilution effect of inflation.

Here you need to make two decisions (See Figure 15-1). First, you need to decide how many years from now you want to retire or to reach financial independence. Second, you need to estimate what the average inflation rate will be between now and that target date.

Over the last 25 years, the inflation rate in the U.S. as expressed by the Department of Labor in the form of the CPI (Consumer Price Index) has been approximately 5.6%. Over the last 10 years it has been 3.7%. One can debate what is an accurate reflection of inflation. However, it is all academic since there is no guarantee that the future will duplicate the past. I will use an average inflation rate of 4.5% for the next 25 years in the examples.

As I described in Step 14, inflation makes things more expensive in the future. Therefore, you must

Figure 15-1: Jodi and Mike's
How Much Does It Take? Worksheet

1. Current need per year = *$51,117*

   60% x *$51,117* = *$30,679*

   (retirement need in TODAY's dollars)

2. Future Value of TODAY's retirement need (4.5%
   inflation; 25 years)

   $$PV = \$30,670$$
   $$N = 25 \ years$$
   $$I = 4.5\%$$
   $$PMT = 0$$
   $$FV = ? = \ \$92,176.67$$

3. Determine inflation-adjusted return
   15% return - (0.5% + 4.5% inflation rate)

   15% - (0.5% + 4.5% inflation rate) =
   15% - 5% =
   10%

4. $/year future value ÷ $/year in chart =
   $1.01 million needed

   $92,177 ÷ $90,909 = $1.01 million

consider the cost of future expenses after inflation. To anticipate what these future inflated prices will be, you must understand the concepts of *present value* and *future value* of money.

The following is a brief description of how to make *future value* projections with a financial calculator. All of my calculations are made on the Hewlett Packard 10B.1*

The present value (PV) of money is the actual amount of money you have today. The future value (FV) of money is what something will be worth in the future. This can be the amount of money you want to accumulate as your goal in the future; the future value of something after inflation has diluted its value; or the amount of money you will need to accumulate to offset the ravages of inflation.

When you use a financial calculator, there are five stroke keys you must understand. The first two I have explained—PV and FV. Another key is the payment key (PMT). This is the dollar amount you can invest periodically. I will use annual payments and projections in the examples. The PMT will also be used later to determine how much you need to

---

*Several financial calculators are available whose manuals describe this concept well and which make calculations as easy as adding a group of numbers. Two calculators which are inexpensive and readily available are the Hewlett Packard 10B and the Texas Instruments BA35.

invest to reach your target financial goal. A fourth key is the interest key (I). This is the *inflation rate* in this example or the *compounding interest rate* I will describe in Step 16. The last key, (N), is the number of years before you reach your goal.

Jodi and Mike anticipate their future yearly expenses to be $30,670. They project this 25 years into the future using 4.5% as an inflation rate.

Using a financial calculator, you will first press the appropriate number keys and then the appropriate function key (N, I, PV, PMT, FV).

For Jodi and Mike, they are: 25 is N; 4.5 is I; 30670 is PV; 0 is PMT; and FV is the unknown. After entering the first four known variables, press the FV key. The answer appears as -92,176.67.

The reason for the negative sign in front of the FV is a function of the calculator. Conceptually, think of everything you put into your investment as a *positive* sign and everything you remove from your investment as a *negative* sign.

Jodi and Mike will require approximately $92,177 The First Year of Retirement 25 years from now to maintain their lifestyle of today.

Inflation is a critical ingredient to incorporate into your future planning!

3. Determine what you believe is reasonable to earn on your invested money, and then adjust it for inflation.

The investment plan I describe in Step 16 will help you determine what is reasonable to expect regarding average compounded returns on your investments. For now use 15%. In Step 16 you will see that this is a reasonable expectation. To adjust investment returns for inflation you have to consider what the real rate of return would be after the dilution effect of inflation is removed. The formula to calculate this is complex:

$$\left[\left(\frac{1 + \text{rate of return}}{1 + \text{rate of inflation}} \right) - 1 \right] \times 100 =$$

$$\left[\left(\frac{1 + .15}{1 + .045} \right) - 1 \right] \times 100 =$$

$$[(1.10048) - 1] \times 100 =$$

$$(0.10048) \times 100 = 10.048\%$$

10.048% = adjusted rate of return

A simplified and fairly accurate method is to subtract (0.5% + the expected inflation rate) from the expected rate of return. This approximates the result of the complex formula. Here is how it works for Jodi and Mike:

In Mike and Jodi's example, the result would be 15% - (0.5% + 4.5%) = 10%. Therefore, the inflation adjusted rate of return is 10%. The only reason you need to calculate the "adjusted rate of return" is to complete the next calculation.

4. Calculate what you must accumulate in the future to live the lifestyle you have chosen upon retirement.

Jodi and Mike have determined that in 25 years they will need a minimum of $92,177 the first year they retire—approximately $7,680 a month. They will also need to increase that amount each year by the inflation rate in order to continue to live their desired lifestyle. Assuming they want their nest egg to last indefinitely, here is how they calculate what they must accumulate between now and retirement.

From the How Long Will It Last? table (see Figure 15-2), locate the column with the interest rate equal to the inflation adjusted rate you calculated in step 3. Mike and Jodi's is 10%. (If your investment plan will change after retirement, and you anticipate a different rate of return, you will need to use that return adjusted for inflation in this calculation.) Then go down the left column labeled *years to withdraw* until you reach the number of years you want your nest egg to last. The number in the space where the *rate of return* column intersects the *years to withdraw* row is how much you can withdraw a year from a $1 million portfolio.

Jodi and Mike are very conservative and in this calculation plan not to deplete their nest egg. Therefore, they will go down to the infinity row (∞) and can withdraw $90,909 a year.

Next, divide the annual dollar amount needed the first year of retirement by the number in the table, and you will have the amount in million-dollars that you must accumulate by retirement in order to live the lifestyle you desire.

For Jodi and Mike, they divide $92,177 by $90,909. They will need to accumulate $1.01 million by retirement to satisfy their projected future needs.

Wow! That is a lot of arithmetic! But, it gets you to the point where you have some educated idea as to where you are going and why. Remember, these projections are not carved in stone. They can be recalculated as your needs dictate. Don't ever feel that you cannot make changes. Be flexible but determined. (There is a blank worksheet in Figure 15-3, for you to use.)

Step 16 is the real *how to* part of the investment process. There I describe the details of the investment plan. Let's get into it.

Figure 15-2: How Long Will It Last?
$1,000,000 Accumulated Wealth

Compounded Annual Rate of Return & Annual Withdrawal*

Years to Withdraw	6%	7%	8%	9%	10%	11%	12%	13%	14%
21	80193	86251	92438	98731	105113	111566	118072	124614	131180
22	78345	84491	90770	97161	103641	110192	116795	123433	130091
23	76678	82910	89280	95763	102338	108983	115679	122406	129150
24	75169	81485	87943	94516	101182	107916	114700	121512	128336
25	73799	80197	86740	93400	100153	106973	113839	120731	127630
26	72551	79029	85655	92399	99235	106137	113082	120048	127018
27	71412	77968	84674	91500	98416	105396	112414	119451	126485
28	70370	77002	83786	90690	97683	104736	111825	118926	126021
29	69415	76120	82980	89959	97026	104149	111304	118467	125618

30	68537	75314	82248	89299	96436	103626	110843	118063	125266
31	67729	74577	81581	88702	95906	103159	110434	117707	124958
32	66983	73900	80973	88162	95429	102742	110072	117395	124690
33	66295	73279	80418	87671	94999	102369	109750	117119	124456
34	65659	72707	79911	87226	94612	102035	109465	116877	124251
35	65070	72181	79447	86822	94263	101736	109211	116663	124072
36	64523	71697	79023	86454	93948	101469	108986	116474	123915
37	64016	71249	78634	86120	93664	101229	108785	116308	123778
38	63545	70837	78277	85815	93406	101014	108607	116161	123658
39	63107	70455	77949	85537	93174	100821	108448	116032	123553
40	62700	70102	77648	85284	92963	100648	108307	115917	123461
X	56604	65421	74074	82569	90909	99099	107143	115044	122807

*Assume that you withdraw what you need for a full year at the beginning of the year and place it in a check-writing money market account. You withdraw your living expenses from this account. Whatever interest you earn on this money is in addition to the annual withdrawal stated in the table.

Figure 15-3: How Much Does It Take?

1. Current need per year: $ _____

60% x $ _____ = $ _____ (retirement need in TODAY'S $)

70% x $ _____ = $ _____ (retirement need in TODAY'S $)

80% x $ _____ = $ _____ (retirement need in TODAY'S $)

90% x $ _____ = $ _____ (retirement need in TODAY'S $)

2. Future value of TODAY's retirement need (____ % inflation; ___ years)

> PV = $ _____
>
> N = ____ years
>
> I = ____ %
>
> PMT = 0
>
> FV = ? = $

3. Determine inflation adjusted return:

> _____ % return - (0.5% + _____ % inflation rate)

4. $ / year future value (from #2 above) ÷ $ / year (from Figure 15-2) =

> $ _____ million needed

$$\frac{\$ \ / \ \text{year} \quad \text{future} \quad \text{value}}{\$ \ / \ \text{year} \quad (\text{from} \quad \text{Figure} \quad 15-2)} = \$ \ _____ \ \text{million needed}$$

16

Have a Plan

You will learn . . .

- *how to create your plan*
- *how to choose no-load mutual funds*
- *the importance of dollar-cost-averaging*
- *how to use the Value Ratio wisely*

When evaluating any plan, I believe that there are four important points to consider: 1. the plan must fit your risk level, time horizon, and goals; 2. the plan must be based on evidence you trust; 3. the plan must make sense to you; 4. the plan must be *simple*. See Figure 16-1.

Many plans work! My plan fits the above criteria and works well for me. It should work well for you too. The basic rules are:

- Know your goals.
- Choose no-load mutual funds which have the best compounded returns over the last 5 year period and are appropriate for your risk level and time horizon.
- Set up your account either directly with the fund company or through a discount broker.

Figure 16-1: Good Plans Are Simple

S Set Goals

I Implement Plan

M Monitor Results

P Provide For Yourself & Family

L Live Without Financial Fear

E Enjoy The Harvest Of Your Efforts

- Invest monthly by dollar-cost-averaging.
- Reduce your exposure in your mutual funds when the Value Ratio is severely overvalued.
- Increase your exposure in your mutual funds when the Value Ratio is severely undervalued.

Know Your Goals

In Step 2, you began to think about your goals. You also learned how to use the When & How form to write down your goals in very specific terms. By the end of Step 16, you will know the exact words to use to complete that form.

All of us have many financial goals. They may include purchasing a first home, saving for a child's college education, investing for retirement, etc. Each goal will be reached in the future. A first home may be 3 years away, a child's college education 12 years away, and a retirement 25 years away. Each goal has its own time horizon and should have its own investment account. Name each separate account for what it is. For example, *New home account, Jane's college account, Jodi's IRA*, etc. To start, you need to know how much to save regularly in order to reach each goal.

For the rest of this discussion, I will describe Jodi and Mike's long-term goal—investing for retirement. However, each of your financial goals can be planned the same way.

*Jodi and Mike are investing for a lifetime. They
want to accumulate enough money within 25 years to
consider themselves financially independent. Following
that, they want to be able to live off their nest egg for
the rest of their lives.*

*In Step 15, they found out how much they had to
accumulate in 25 years to make this happen. This was
based on what they expected their future needs to be,
an investment vehicle compounding annually at 15%
on average, and inflation running around 4.5%. Their
financial goal in 25 years was to accumulate $1.01
million. What they needed to know now was how they
would get there—how much they needed to save regularly. They used a financial calculator to make the
following necessary calculations.*

• *Mike and Jodi know their financial goal is to
accumulate $1,010,000. They enter 1,010,000 into the
calculator and then change the sign to negative (-).
(Remember, negative means you "take away" and
positive means you "put into". In 25 years, Jodi and
Mike will "take away" $1,010,000.) They then press
the FV key.*

• *Since Jodi and Mike will be investing for 25
years in order to reach this goal, they enter 25 and
press the N key.*

• *The annual compounded interest they hope to
realize is 15%. They enter 15 and press the I key.*

• At this point, they are each starting with $500 in their IRAs for a combined total of $1,000.00. Therefore, they enter 1,000 and press the PV key.

• The unknown is their annual investment payments (PMT). (Since these payments will be made at the beginning of each year, the financial calculator must be set for "Begin" payment mode. See calculator instructions). They press the PMT key and the answer appears as $3,992.78. (Both Jodi and Mike are employed and can contribute a maximum of $2,000 each to their own IRAs.)

$3,992.78 (or approximately $4,000) is the annual dollar amount Jodi and Mike must invest at 15% for 25 years to reach their target of $1.01 million. Can they do it? Absolutely! Follow along with me.

Choose Fund Categories

In Step 13, you took your financial temperature to determine what type of investor you are. You cannot become a successful investor unless you know this critically basic fact. See Figure 16-2.

Jodi and Mike decided they registered "growth-oriented" on the financial thermometer (see Step 13). They believe that they could sleep easily at night even if their investment over a period of 12 months would fluctuate down as much as 25%. But, they also realize that they are only comfortable at this

Figure 16-2: Investment Thermometer

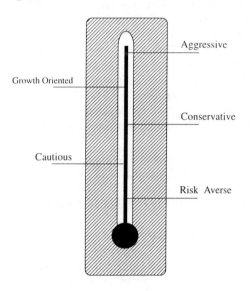

• Starting With A $10,000 Investment •

If you can accept a fluctuation   Then your *investment temperature*
over a one year period of...   for this investment goal is...

0% (no loss of principal) .... Risk averse

up to 5% drop (up to $500) .... Cautious

up to 15% drop (up to $1,500) .... Conservative

up to 25% drop (up to $2,500) .... Growth-Oriented

over 25% drop (over $2,500) .... Aggressive

*level because they know that the trend of the stock
market over the long-term is "up" and that 25 years is
a long time during which most risk is greatly
"smoothed out."*

Jodi and Mike can determine the appropriate
fund categories for their investment temperature by
referring to the chart we saw first in Step 13 titled
How to Choose Fund Categories. See Table 16-1.

*Under the fund category "Growth-Oriented", Jodi
and Mike go across to the column labeled "Time Horizon over 7 years." Their ideal investment categories
are Growth funds, International stock funds, and
International bond funds.*

*Remember, they can also invest in any category
less risky than Growth-Oriented and a shorter
horizon.*

How do you know which funds to choose within
these categories? Here's how . . .

Select Specific Funds

Successful funds over the last 5 years tend to stay
successful; unsuccessful funds over the last 5 years
tend to remain unsuccessful. Various scholarly
investigators have shown this to be true. Our task
is to determine which funds have been historically
the most successful over the previous 5 year period.

One source I use to determine the best performing funds is an annual book *The Individual Investor's*

Table 16-1: How To Choose Fund Categories

Investment Temperature	Time Horizon			
	Up to 2 yrs.	2-4 yrs.	4-7 yrs.	Over 7 yrs.
Risk Averse	(Money market funds; actual purchase of U.S. Treasury securities* and zero-coupon bonds** for specific time horizon)			
Cautious	Money Market	Short-term Bond	Interm.-term Bond	Long-term Bond
Conservative	Money Market	Short-term Bond	Balanced	Growth & Income
			Interm.-term Bond	Long-term Bond

	Money Market	Short-term Bond	Growth	Growth
Growth Oriented			International Stock International Bond	International Stock International Bond
Aggressive	Money Market	Short-term Bond	Aggressive Growth Gold Stock Sector	Aggressive Growth Gold Stock Sector

* U.S. Treasury securities: These are negotiable debt obligations of the U.S. government, secured by its full faith and credit and issued at various schedules and maturities. The income from Treasury securities is exempt from state and local, but not federal, taxes.

** Zero Coupon bonds: These bonds make no periodic interest payments. They are sold at a deep discount from its face value. The buyer of this bond receives the total accumulated rate of return when the bond is redeemed on a specific maturity date. For tax purposes, the IRS maintains that the holder of the zero coupon bond owes income tax on the interest that has accrued each year, even though the bond holder does not actually receive the cash until maturity.

Guide to Low-Load Mutual Funds and its *Mutual Fund Quarterly Update* newsletter published by the American Association of Individual Investors, a non-profit organization (312-280-0170). AAII also offers an excellent monthly journal, seminars, and membership. Another excellent source is *Morningstar No-Load Funds*, a monthly resource (800-876-5005).

I have compiled two lists from these sources. The first list (see Table 16-2) identifies the two best performing no-load funds for each category of funds over the last five years. The second list (see Table 16-3) identifies all the no-load mutual funds that have average compounded returns of 15% or greater over the previous ten year period.

To gather the data yourself from *The Individual Investors Guide to Low-Load Mutual Funds*, refer to the *"Fund Performance Rankings"* chapter. (Both no-load and low-load funds are followed in this reference book. I only include the no-load funds here.) In *Morningstar No-Load Funds*, refer to *"Summary Section, Issue B"*.

Now, getting back to Jodi and Mike:

Jodi and Mike's chosen fund categories are Growth funds, International stock funds, and International bond funds. From the "Top 2 Funds of Each Category," Jodi and Mike select from: Meridian, Brandywine, Lexington Worldwide Emerging, Warburg Pincus International Equities, Scudder International Bonds, and T. Rowe Price International

*Bond. Of these, Meridian also appears in the "15% &
Greater 10-Year Total Returns" list.*

Once you determine the funds that fit your
criteria, you need to obtain the necessary information about each fund, make your final choices, and
set up your accounts.

Set Up Account

Contact the fund companies you are interested in.
Use "800" phone numbers listed for your conve-
nience. Request 1. a prospectus, 2. the most recent
quarterly or annual reports, and 3. an application
for the type of account you are opening (general,
IRA, etc.).

The prospectus is a detailed document. It will
identify the fund's specific objectives, its style of
investing, the risks involved, and the overall opera-
tion of the fund.

The quarterly or annual report will be easier to
read than the prospectus. It will generally have the
fund manager's opinion about market conditions,
how the fund is exploiting these conditions, and
how the fund is expected to do in the future. There
will also be a discussion of the recent performance
of the fund, a list of all the securities in the fund,
and the fund's financial statement. Read through
the prospectus and reports. Be sure that each fund

Table 16-2: Top 2 Funds of Each Category

5 year compounded total returns through 8/31/94

sources: Mutual Fund Quarterly Update; Morningstar No-Load Funds

Type	Name	Phone #	Price ($)	5 Year
Aggressive Growth				
	Crabbe Huson Special	800-541-9732	$13.78	18.0%
	PBHG	800-809-8008	$14.69	20.0%
Growth				
	Meridian	800-446-6662	$25.88	15.1%
	Brandywine	302-656-6200	$24.74	15.8%
Growth & Income				
	Safeco Equity	800-426-6730	$14.47	14.1%
	Schafer Value	800-343-0481	$37.99	13.4%
Balanced				
	CGM Mutual	800-345-4048	$27.33	12.0%
	Invesco Industrial Income	800-525-8085	$11.75	13.7%
Bond: Taxable				
Short-Term				
	Strong Advantage	800-368-1030	$10.04	7.5%
	Dreyfus Short/Int. Gov't	800-645-6561	$10.86	8.2%
Intermediate-Term				
	Fidelity Capital & Income	800-544-8888	$9.14	12.3%
	Northeast Investors	800-225-6704	$9.96	10.7%

Long-Term

Vanguard Long-Term Corp.	800-662-7447	$8.36	9.8%
Fidelity Investment Grade	800-544-8888	$7.12	9.5%

Bond: Tax Exempt

Short-Term

Dreyfus Short/Int.-Term Muni.	800-645-6561	$12.97	6.1%
Vanguard Limited-Term Muni.	800-662-7447	$10.57	6.5%

Intermediate-Term

Vanguard PA Tax Free	800-662-7447	$10.84	8.8%
Vanguard NY Insured Tax Free	800-662-7447	$10.46	8.5%

Long-Term

General NY Muni Bond	800-645-6561	$19.71	8.7%
Vanguard Muni. High Yield	800-662-7447	$10.39	8.9%

International Stock

Lexington Worldwide Emerging	800-526-0056	$13.73	12.4%
Warburg Pincus Int'l Equity	800-257-5614	$20.89	15.3%

International Bond

Scudder International Bond	800-225-2470	$11.87	13.0%
T. Rowe Price Int'l Bond	800-638-5660	$9.64	11.4%

Gold

United Services World Gold	800-873-8637	$16.37	5.5%
Benham Gold Equities Index	800-321-8321	$12.35	5.5%

Sector

Invesco Strategic - Financial	800-525-8085	$16.01	19.7%
Invesco Strategic - Technology	800-525-8085	$23.67	21.0%

Figure 16-3: 15% & Greater 10-Year Total Returns through 8/31/94

Source: Morningstar No-Load Mutual Funds

Name	Category	Phone #	Price ($)	10 Year
Acorn	Aggressive	800-922-6769	$13.58	17.5%
Berger 100	Growth	800-333-1001	$15.79	18.4%
Century Shares	Sector-Financial	800-321-1928	$23.74	15.1%
CGM Capital Development	Growth	800-345-4048	$25.98	21.9%
CGM Mutual	Balanced	800-345-4048	$27.33	16.5%
Dodge & Cox Stock	Growth & Income		$56.86	16.1%
Fidelity Retirement Growth	Growth	800-544-8888	$18.68	16.2%
Founders Growth	Growth	800-525-2440	$12.25	15.5%
IAI Regional	Growth	800-945-3863	$20.93	16.1%
Invesco Industrial Income	Growth & Income	800-525-8085	$11.75	16.6%
Invesco Pacific Basin	Foreign Stock	800-525-8085	$17.03	15.5%
Invesco Strategic Health	Sector-Health	800-525-8085	$34.58	20.0%
Invesco Strategic Leisure	Sector	800-525-8085	$22.42	20.0%
Invesco Strategic Technology	Sector-Technology	800-525-8085	$23.67	17.0%
Janus	Growth	800-525-3713	$19.76	15.4%

Japan	Foreign Stock	800-225-2470	$12.43	16.4%
Lexington Corporate Leaders	Growth & Income	800-526-0056	$11.09	15.3%
Managers Capital Appreciation	Growth	800-835-3879	$25.71	15.3%
Meridian	Growth	800-446-6662	$25.88	15.3%
Mutual Beacon	Growth & Income	800-448-3863	$33.86	15.8%
Mutual Qualified	Growth & Income	800-448-3863	$29.18	16.0%
Mutual Shares	Growth & Income	800-488-3863	$86.61	15.6%
Neuberger & Berman Guardian	Growth & Income	800-877-9700	$19.52	15.4%
T. Rowe Price Int'l Stock	Foreign Stock	800-638-5660	$12.93	18.8%
Safeco Equity	Growth & Income	800-426-6730	$14.47	16.5%
Scudder International Stock	Foreign Stock	800-225-2470	$45.07	16.9%
Sequoia	Growth	212-245-4500	$59.02	15.4%
Stein Roe Special	Growth	800-338-2550	$23.67	16.0%
20th Century Giftrust Investors	Aggressive	800-345-2021	$17.64	23.4%
20th Century Growth Investors	Growth	800-345-2021	$22.77	15.7%
Vanguard International Growth	Foreign Stock	800-662-7447	$14.36	17.8%
Vanguard Spec. Health Care	Sector-Health	800-662-7447	$37.19	20.4%
Vanguard Trustees' Equity Int'l	Foreign Stock	800-662-7447	$34.09	17.3%
Vanguard Windsor	Growth & Income	800-662-7447	$14.77	15.1%

you are researching meets your specific needs and risk level.

Next open your investment accounts. Complete the application, make out a check to the fund, and mail all the required documents. Be sure to *check off* that you want telephone switching privileges. This allows you to call the fund to request your fund shares to be sold and switched to the money market account and vice versa as you see fit. Also *check off* that all dividends and capital gains are reinvested. This is offered by all mutual funds and enhances compounding. (Remember what happened to Christopher Columbus's penny through the wonder of compounding!)

You could open an account with each individual mutual fund company in which you want to invest, or you could use the services of a discount broker to handle all of your transactions with all the different fund companies.

There are many discount brokers who allow you to buy and sell no-load mutual funds either for a very low transaction fee or no transaction fee. Here is a list (see Table 16-4). (When there is no transaction fee, the mutual fund has arranged to pay the discount broker a commission out of its operating expenses.)

Using a discount broker makes life very simple because with only one phone call everything is handled for you. Many brokers are open 24 hours a day, 7 days a week, to take your orders personally—not by recording devices!

To establish your account(s) with a discount broker, call the brokerage firm and request information on their mutual fund investing program. Tell them what types of accounts you want to establish such as general investing, IRA, trust, etc. Also request a prospectus for each of the funds in which you are interested.

When you return your brokerage account application form, include your initial check which will be deposited into a money market fund. You can then call the brokerage company and request that specific dollar amounts be invested among your choice of mutual funds.

If you have several existing accounts with different fund families already, you may be able to have them all transferred to one discount broker. And, the discount broker will take care of the transfers for you. Call the discount broker to request the appropriate paperwork.

Jodi and Mike decided to use a discount broker. They made their phone call and requested all of the pertinent information. They decided they would invest in different funds purchased through the broker with no transaction fees charged. Mike and Jodi both transferred their existing IRA to the broker. Each has $2,000 to invest—the annual maximum for an IRA. To reach their goal of $3,994 a year each must

Table 16-4: Discount Brokers

AccuTrade	800-228-3011	Muriel Siebert	800-872-0711
Andrew Peck	800-221-5873	New England Investment	800-472-7227
Arnold Securities	800-328-4076	PC Financial Network	800-825-5723
Aufhauser & Co.	800-368-3668	Quick & Reilly	800-221-5220
Baltimore BanCorp Invest	800-634-4935	Robert Thomas	800-242-1523
Barry Murphy & Co.	800-221-2111	S.C. Costa Co.	918-582-0110
Bidwell & Co.	800-547-6337	Seaport Securities Corp.	800-732-7678
Broker's Exchange	800-476-3738	Securities Research	800-327-3156
Bruno, Stolze & Co.	800-899-6878	Shearman, Ralston	800-221-4242
Bull & Bear Securities	800-262-5800	Spear Securities	800-455-2211
Calvert Securities Corp.	800-999-3699	Sterling Investment	800-782-1522
Charles Schwab	800-435-4000	T. Rowe Price Discount	800-638-5660

CoreStates Securities	800-222-0124
Downstate Discount	813-586-3541
Fidelity Brokerage Services	800-544-8666
First Institutional Securities	800-526-7486
Fleet Brokerage Securities	800-221-8210
Freeman Welwood & Co.	800-729-7585
J.D. Seibert & Co.	800-247-3396
Jack White & Co.	800-233-3411
Lombard Institutional	800-688-3462
Marsh Block & Co.	800-366-1500
Max Ule	800-223-6642
Mongerson & Co.	800-621-2627
Thomas F. White	800-669-4483
Tuttle Securities	800-962-5489
U.J.B. Investor Services	800-631-1635
Unified Brokerage System	800-862-7283
Waterhouse Securities	800-934-4410
White Discount Securities	800-700-6363
Wisconsin Discount	414-352-5050
York Securities	800-221-3154
Your Discount Broker	800-800-3215

invest at least $1,997 a year. However, they will each contribute their maximum $2,000 per year into their IRA plans. This will actually net them slightly more than they calculated their retirement goal to be. Beginning next year, they plan to send monthly checks to the broker and have them invested into the no-transaction-fee mutual funds they have selected.

Dollar-Cost-Average

Dollar-cost-averaging is the secret ingredient to wealth accumulation. Think of this as the high-test gasoline that keeps the finely tuned engine running smoothly. It is critical for your success.

Once you have determined how much you must invest annually to reach your goal, divide the amount by 12, and you have your necessary monthly investment. By investing the same dollar amount regularly, you are dollar-cost-averaging. Dollar-cost-averaging is the best way to invest over the long-term. You purchase fewer shares when the price is high and more shares when the price is low.

The method of dollar-cost-averaging also creates investment discipline—a trait well worth acquiring.

If you feel you may forget to invest monthly, consider any of these three options:

1. Pay all of your bills once a month and make your investment the *first* bill you pay; or

2. Arrange for your fund to send you a monthly reminder notice; or

3. Arrange for your fund to automatically draft your savings or checking account monthly.

Determine the Value Ratio; Use it Wisely

As I discussed in Step 12, the Value Ratio can help you identify when the U.S. stock market is overvalued or undervalued. The Value Ratio is the price per dividend ratio of the S&P 500 Index. It is simple to interpret (see Figure 16-3).

Over the last century, the Value Ratio has been above 34.00 only 5% of the time and below 15.00 only 6% of the time. When above 34.00, the resulting stock market correction averaged a 41% drop! When below 15.00, the resulting stock market advance averaged a 240% rise! These are startling statistics which should open up your eyes!

You can use the Value Ratio as an upper and lower boundary line. Whenever the Value Ratio rises above 34.00, consider shifting some or all of your investment dollars out of your stock funds and into the safety of a money market fund.

Don't begin to move this cash back into the stock funds until the Value Ratio drops below 30.00. At

Figure 16-3: Value Ratio

If the Value Ratio* is:		Then the U.S. Market is:
> 34.00		severely overvalued
30.00 - 34.00		overvalued
20.00 - 30.00	↔	average
15.00 - 20.00		undervalued
< 15.00		severely undervalued

*The Value Ratio has been popularized by Walter Rouleau. Growth Fund Research Inc., Box 6600, Rapid City, SD 57709.

that point, begin dollar-cost-averaging back into the stock funds over a period of several months.

Whenever the Value Ratio is below 15.00, consider switching some of your invested dollars into more aggressive funds. The aggressive fund category tends to outperform the rest of the stock market when the market is in an uptrend.

This little effort on your part could improve your overall total returns by a few percentage points which can be very significant over the long-term.

Here's how Jodi and Mike could benefit by simply improving their total return by 1%, 2%, or 3% respectively.

Jodi and Mike have a total starting value of $1,000 in their IRAs ($500 each). At 15% compounded a year and a total of $4,000 invested at the beginning of each year, Jodi and Mike's accounts will accumulate to approximately a total of $1,012,000 in 25 years. At 16%, they will grow to approximately $1,197,000. At 17%, the accounts shoot up to $1,418,000. At 18%, their nest egg explodes to $1,680,000! By earning only 3% above their projected 15% compounded return, they can accumulate approximately $668,000 more money by the time they reach retirement! There is a great deal to be gained by simply improving the total return by just a few percentage points!

It is *simple to do.* The Value Ratio is calculated once a week on Friday. If Friday is a holiday, use the last trading day of the week.

The Value Ratio is calculated by dividing the S&P 500 Index by the dividends paid for those stocks in that Index over the previous 52 weeks.

The "S&P 500 Index" and "dividends paid" can be found weekly in *Barron's Financial Newspaper.* Go to the "Market Week" pull-out section and then open to "Barron's Market Laboratory." The "S&P 500 Index" is listed in the column called "Other Market Indexes" (usually located in the bottom left hand corner of the second page of the "Laboratory" section). The "dividends paid" is listed in the column called "Indexes' P/Es & Yields" (usually located in the top left-hand corner of the third page of the "Laboratory" section) under the S&P 500 subheading as "Divs, $". The following is an example from a 1994 issue of *Barron's*. Here is how the calculation for the Value Ratio for this date works out.

Formula:

Value Ratio = S&P 500 Index ÷ Dividends for previous 52 weeks

S&P 500 Index = 473.77
Dividends paid = 13.08
Value Ratio = 473.77 ÷ 13.08 = 36.22

Use the following table (see Table 16-4) to keep track of the Value Ratios.

I know this was a difficult step to absorb all at one time. It was difficult for me to write. I had to make sure that my 23-year-old son could understand it before I would be satisfied with it. He did; so, I was.

Without a doubt, you may need to reread this step several times before it really *sinks in*. But, once you've got it, you can complete your When & How form with ease. Then you can start your plan. (See how Jodi and Mike have filled out their When & How form for their retirement plan in Figure 16-5.)

Don't get overwhelmed by all the technical *lingo*. The more you play with the numbers, the more familiar it will become. Making the decision to take control of your financial future is a major commitment. It takes some effort. But, if you are serious about wanting to achieve financial independence in the not so distant future, then bite the bullet, and get started *now*! (If you have any questions, you can write me, and I will reply. My mailing address is: P.O. Box 30548, Charleston, SC 29417-0548.)

Congratulations! You have just completed over 75% of the puzzle.

You will now need to keep your plan healthy. Preventive medicine keeps a healthy body on track by *monitoring* its physical and mental health. In a similar way, *preventive medicine* keeps your financial health on track by *monitoring* your financial plan. Chapter 17 will show you the way!

Take a break. Go see a good movie! Then, we'll meet again in Step 17.

Figure 16-4: Tracking the Value Ratio

$$\text{Value Ratio} \quad = \quad \frac{\text{S \& P 500 Stock Index}}{\text{Dividends paid over previous 52 weeks}}$$

Date	S&P 500	Div.	VR

Date	S&P 500	Div.	VR

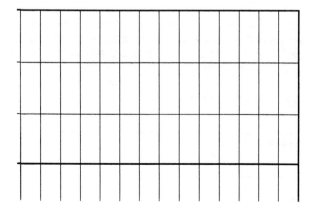

Figure 16-5: When & How: Jodi and Mike's Retirement Goal

GOAL?

Financial Independence—accumulate $1.01 million

WHEN?

Jodi and Mike will retire financially independent in 25 years.

HOW?

We will begin with $500 in each of our IRAs. We will each invest $2,000 a year, for a total of $4,000 yearly, divided into monthly contributions, into no-load mutual funds within our IRA accounts over the next 25 years. We will select the best performing funds over the previous 5 year periods. These funds will be in the categories which fit our investment temperature—namely Growth stock funds, International stock funds, and International bond funds. Our goal is to average an annually-compounded total return of 15%. We will also monitor the Value Ratio and the success of our funds, and we will make adjustments as necessary.

_____   _____

signature   date

_____   _____

signature   date

17

Monitor Your Success

You will learn . . .

* *a unique method to track your investment growth*

Monitoring your journey toward financial security will not only help you visualize how your *plan* is progressing, but will also alert you of any problems along the way.

Here is a simple but extremely useful tool to monitor each of your financial goals. For this, you will compute a few target dollar values quickly with the use of your financial calculator.

The Annual Monitor table projects what the values of your account should be for a specific financial goal at the end of each year. It succinctly monitors where you are and where you should be. If you are off track, you will be made aware of that quickly. How to resolve this problem is discussed in Step 18.

The following explains the terms used in the Annual Monitor (see Figure 17-1).

Goal: This is the amount of money you wish to accumulate at a specific time in the future for a particular financial goal. This is the FV button on the financial calculator. [Remember, this will be a negative (-) number.]

Years to reach goal: This is the number of years you have to allow compounding and your plan to work for you before reaching your *Goal*. This is the N button on the financial calculator.

Beginning value of portfolio: This is the amount of money, if any, you are starting with. This is the PV button on the financial calculator and begins at the *End of Year "0".*

Anticipated annually-compounded rate of return: There is no guarantee you will achieve this return. It is based on the historical returns of the funds you choose. It is always wise to underestimate this number. This is the I button on the financial calculator.

Annual contribution: This is the sum of money you will be able to contribute, or the sum of money you must contribute, into your investment plan to reach your *Goal*. You can invest this amount monthly, quarterly, or however you wish. For simplicity, the calculation is based on this amount being added annually at the *beginning* of each year. Your first regular contribution will be invested at the beginning of year "1". This is the PMT button on the financial calculator.

End of Year: All calculations are based on the value of the account at the end of the year. When determining the *Target* value, this is the N button on the financial calculator.

End of: This is the end of the year you actually are targeting.

Age: This is your age at the end of the *Target* year.

Target: This is the dollar amount your portfolio should be worth if you are on track with your *Goal*. This is the FV button on the financial calculator.

Actual: This is the real value of your portfolio at the end of the *Target* year. If you have a *Beginning value of portfolio*, this dollar amount is entered into the *Actual* column for the *End of Year "0"*. You will fill in the actual value of your portfolio as you monitor this form each year.

Adjustments: This is the difference between the *Actual* amount minus the *Target* amount. If this is a negative number when you monitor this form, you need to consider making an adjustment to your plan. (This is discussed in Step 18.) If you have more in your plan than is targeted, consider this as a cushion against future years which may not be as successful.

Let's revisit Jodi and Mike and fill out their Annual Monitor table for their retirement goal. I'll complete Jodi's table (see Figure 17-2) for her IRA which will be an exact duplicate of Mike's IRA.

At the end of 1995 (year "0"), Jodi is starting with $500. At the beginning of 1996, she will begin her investment program. To simplify the calculations, I'll assume that her annual investments of $2,000 are

Figure 17:1: Annual Monitor of Financial Success

Date ————

GOAL ————

Years to reach goal ————

Beginning value of portfolio ————

Anticipated annually-compounded rate of return ————

Annual contribution ————

End of Year	End of	Age	Target	Actual	Adjustments
0					
1					
2					
3					
4					
5					

	6	7	8	9	10	11	12	13	14	15	16	17	18	19

Figure 17-1: Annual Monitor of Financial Success (*continued*)

End of Year	End of	Age	Target	Actual	Adjustments
20					
21					
22					
23					
24					
25					
26					
27					
28					
29					
30					
31					

32	33	34	35	36	37	38	39	40	41	42	43	44	45	46

Figure 17-2: Annual Monitor for Jodi's IRA

Date _____

GOAL _____ $505,000

Years to reach goal _____ 25

Beginning value of portfolio _____ $500

Anticipated annually-compounded rate of return _____ 15%

Annual contribution _____ $2,000

End of Year	End of	Age	Target	Actual	Adjustments
0	1995	30		$500	
1	1996	31	$2,875		
2	1997	32	$5,606		
3	1998	33	$8,747		
4	1999	34	$12,359		
5	2000	35	$16,513		

6	2001	36	$21,290				
7	2002	37	$26,784				
8	2003	38	$33,101				
9	2004	39	$40,366				
10	2005	40	$48,721				
11	2006	41	$58,330				
12	2007	42	$69,379				
13	2008	43	$82,086				
14	2009	44	$96,699				
15	2010	45	$113,503				
16	2011	46	$132,829				
17	2012	47	$155,053				
18	2013	48	$180,611				
19	2014	49	$210,003				

Figure 17-2: Annual Monitor for Jodi's IRA *(continued)*

End of Year	End of	Age	Target	Actual	Adjustments
20	2015	50	$243,804		
21	2016	51	$282,674		
22	2017	52	$327,375		
23	2018	53	$378,781		
24	2019	54	$437,899		
25	2020	55	$505,883		
26					
27					
28					
29					
30					
31					
32					

33	34	35	36	37	38	39	40	41	42	43	44	45	46

all deposited at the beginning of each year rather than divided over the 12 month period. (Since payments are made at the beginning of each payment period, be sure to set the financial calculator "payment mode" to BEGIN.)

At the "end of year 1", Jodi should have $500 plus $2,000 plus 15% total investment return ($375) to equal $2,875. To determine the target balance, enter "1" and then press the N key; enter "500" and then press the PV key; enter "15" and then press the I key; enter "2,000" and then press the PMT key. Press the FV key to get the "target value at the end of year 1" ($2,875).

Do this for all 25 years. Simply press 2; press N; press FV; and you have the value at the "end of year 2". Press 3; press N; press FV; and you have the value at the "end of year 3", etc. You won't have to reenter the numbers for I, PV, or PMT. They are already in the calculator.

The Annual Monitor will fill in as shown in the example in Figure 17-2. That's all there is to it.

The blank Annual Monitor table in Figure 17-1 is for you to use. Save your table along with all of your other important papers. Each year, complete the Actual column and determine if you are staying on track. If not, adjustments may be necessary.

Turn to Step 18. There you will find several ideas about how to make adjustments to your plan as needed.

18

Adjust Your Plan as Necessary

You will learn . . .

• *various options to help you stay on track with your financial goals*

As you progress toward your financial goal, your Annual Monitor will show you if you are on track. If you have more in your account than is targeted, consider this a cushion against future years which may not be as successful. If you have less than is targeted, you may need to make some adjustments. Here are some options to keep you on target.

Add More to Your Plan

By monitoring your plan annually, you will be able to catch discrepancies early. If you are *down* an amount that is affordable for you to add to your account, do it. If this is an IRA or other qualified retirement account, you are limited to the maximum dollars you can add per year. What you could do is open up a low-fee variable annuity as discussed in Step 9 or open up a regular account with your chosen mutual fund.

Switch to Better Performing Funds

If any of your funds are not performing well, consider switching to a better performing fund. If your account is not in a tax-deferred vehicle, then there will be tax consequences to consider when switching funds. However, your priority should be quality investment returns; taxes should hold second place.

Review the latest issue of *Morningstar No-Load Funds* or *The Individual Investor's Guide to Low-Load Mutual Funds.* It is best to monitor either of these two resources at least once a year to be able to fine tune your plan. Identify the best performing funds over the last five years within your fund categories. If they are also on the *15% or Greater 10-Year Total Returns* list, all the better.

If you need to switch funds, obtain a prospectus of the new fund and a transfer form. The new fund can handle the transfer for you with minimal hassles. If you are using a discount broker, the transfer can be done with just one telephone call.

Change Dollar Value of Goal

Possibly you can decrease the projected amount of your goal. For example, if you are trying to accumulate $50,000 for a particular financial goal, but

$40,000 would still work, then this may be a viable option.

Change Projected Date to Reach Goal

If you have some flexibility in your time frame, then you may want to extend your goal date. This additional time will give your plan added compounding power to grow toward your target value.

•

The light at the end of the tunnel is getting closer! Can you feel the excitement of accomplishing your goal? If you can't just yet, you will. It is a very satisfying feeling to know that you are taking control of your financial destiny.

When you have control of your financial destiny, you are living without financial fear, and you will be providing for yourself and your family. *Remember: No one cares more about your money than you!* Never forget that!

19

Teach Your Children About Money

You will learn . . .

- *seven hot tips to teach your children*

Teaching your children early about money will help them to be more responsible and financially secure adults. This step is not a formal dissertation on the subject of money, but it does lay an important foundation on which to build a solid philosophy. Bottom line: Live within your means. This is the perfect time to teach your children this basic concept of financial responsibility.

I have divided the remainder of Step 19 into seven hot tips for you as parents to pass on to your children or grandchildren. Make learning about money fun!

Hot Tip #1: Teach your children about interest and compounding.

Interest is the cost of holding money. When you borrow money from a bank, you pay interest to the bank for the money until you repay the loan. Likewise, when you put money into a bank savings account, the bank pays you interest for holding your money until you take your money back.

Compounding is the interest earned on previously earned interest which is reinvested with the original principal. Reread the story in Step 6 about Christopher Columbus and his penny.

Many banks have special savings clubs for children to make saving fun. Check this out in your area. Some are called *Squirrel Accounts* or *Acorn Accounts*. Have your child open up one of these accounts. Explain to him or her how regular savings every week can grow through the power of earning interest and compounding. (Your child will need a Social Security card. Call the U.S. Department of Social Security at 800-772-1213 to find out how to apply.)

For example, if Jodi and Mike's daughter Jane puts $5 into her savings account every week, and it earns 5% annual interest compounding weekly, then she will have deposited $260 into the bank in one year. At the end of that year, however, it will be worth about $267. Look at the following chart at the top of the next page to see how Jane's savings account grows over the years with weekly deposits of $5 and compounding at 5%.

One way of encouraging your children to save is to match their deposits with the same amount. In the above example, you could offer to match the $5

In ___ years	Total Deposited	Value of Savings Account
1	$260	$267
5	$1,300	$1,478
10	$2,600	$3,375
15	$3,900	$5,810

your child is saving with $5 for a total of $10 a week. That's a pretty good incentive!

Hot Tip #2: Teach your children how money works by exchanging things of value.

By the age of 3 or 4, most children know about money but don't understand its value. This is a good time to show them what a dime can do in a gumball machine, or a quarter in a pay telephone, or several coins in a vending machine. The importance here is to communicate. For instance, talk about the things that $1 will purchase compared to $5.

Even the youngest children can accumulate some money for doing certain things. For example, you could pay your child for completing specific chores around the house. Or, your child could earn money by taking aluminum cans to be recycled. (Many hardware stores sell *aluminum can crushers* which are inexpensive and safe to use.)

Let your child take this earned money and purchase an item with it that he or she wants. Your child will learn the way money comes into their life in exchange for goods and services and then how it leaves their life again in exchange for goods or services.

This begins to train your child to think before spending. Your child will learn to answer the following questions, "Is the item really what I want?" "Can I purchase it at a lesser price by comparison shopping?" "Should I save this money instead?"

Hot Tip #3: Teach your children the benefits of a budget.

A budget simply helps manage and control one's money. Your Cash Flow Statement from Step 1 shows how you budgeted your money for the previous year. A budget tells you what you can spend in the upcoming year for various categories based on your income.

Let your children see how you budget your household expenses. Let them see how you write checks every month for your fixed and variable expenses. As they become familiar with your monthly ritual of paying bills and balancing your checkbook, they will catch on to the process.

Your children could use envelopes to budget their expenses. They can take their money and allowance and divide it into categories such as savings, toys, school lunch, entertainment, etc.

Help your children set goals. For example, if your daughter wants a bicycle, help her save for it by using a budget, a savings account, and a source of earned income. Let her work at home to earn money to put away for her goal. Once there, she will gain the satisfaction of knowing it is hers. She truly earned it!

Hot Tip #4: Charge your children interest.

Once your children have learned the value of money and are receiving either an allowance and/or money from household chores, they will occasionally spend all of their money before their next *paycheck*. If they need to borrow money from you, advance them a loan, but charge them interest. This will teach them how credit works and how much it costs.

Hot Tip #5: Encourage your children to learn business skills.

The United States is a land where entrepreneurs make opportunities happen! Your children can learn to become *movers and shakers* in the business community. They can make things happen for themselves financially.

Encourage your children to find jobs to earn extra money. Let them create! Support them, and help them work out their problems. Above all, let them know that these jobs are learning experiences which will provide them with the basic skills that they will carry with them for the rest of their lives.

Hot Tip #6: Teach your children about various investment options.

Make a game out of this. Give each of your children $100,000 in play money to purchase various investment vehicles such as stocks, bonds, mutual funds, gold, certificates of deposit, etc. Then, once a month review how well or poorly each portfolio is doing. There is a wealth of learning to be gained by such a game.

Your children will learn about long-term versus short-term investing. They will begin to understand risk and investment temperament. They will also gain an appreciation for wealth accumulation.

You will need to help them learn about the tax laws. What taxes will they have to pay on their investment gains? What will be left for them to keep? These reality lessons will go a long way in educating your children about the real world.

Hot Tip #7: Have your children open up their own Mutual Fund with automatic investing.

This is the real stuff! Give your children an opportunity to open up their own mutual fund. Some funds can be started with as little as $250. The fund can send them reminder notices to encourage them to make regular investments into their account. They will have the thrill of seeing their money grow into something of great value for them.

Here are several no-load mutual funds (see Table 19-1) which can be started with $250 or less. Fund name, category, and phone number are listed. The minimum initial investment (Min.) and minimum subsequent investments (Sub.) are noted. Finally, the annual compounded total return for the past three and five year periods are given as of 8/31/94.

This is the groundwork for your children to become self-sufficient financially. They will grow to appreciate the value of money, the importance of money, and the means of making money. You will be very proud; they will be very appreciative!

Figure 19-1: Funds with $250 Start-Up Costs

Fund Name	Fund Category	Phone #	Min.	Sub.	3 year	5 year
Berger 100	Growth	800-333-1001	$250	$50	13.8%	18.2%
Berger 101	Growth & Income	800-333-1001	$250	$50	13.5%	14.3%
MIM Stock Appreciation	Growth	800-233-1240	$250	$50	8.8%	15.2%
MSB	Growth	212-551-1920	$50	$25	10.2%	8.4%
Muhlenkamp	Growth & Income	800-860-3863	$200	$100	14.7%	10.0%
Pax World	Balanced	800-767-1729	$250	$50	2.2%	7.8%
Strong Investment	Balanced	800-368-1030	$250	$50	8.1%	7.3%
Strong Total Return	Growth & Income	800-368-1030	$250	$50	10.7%	6.2%
20th Century Giftrust	Aggressive Growth	800-345-2021	$250	$50	24.6%	19.3%

20

Help Your Elderly Parents

You will learn . . .

* *potential problems facing your parents in the future*
* *solutions to these problems*

The paradox is that what your parents did for you when you were a child is what you must now consider doing for them as they become elderly. The roles reverse themselves.

And, new financial strains on your parents can place pressure on your continuing journey toward financial security.

Because of the healthier lifestyles we are choosing, life expectancies and the quality of life are dramatically improving. Many of our parents may well live into their 80s, 90s, and beyond. And, although they have probably said, "We don't want to be a burden on you," they will undoubtedly become much more dependent on you as they age. And, most children want to help.

One method to help ease the burden later on is to have an open dialogue now between you and your parents concerning their options for housing, health care, insurance, and financial management. Then later, both of you will be better equipped to tackle most of the difficulties which may arise. Following are some potential problems which could affect your parents.

Difficulty Maintaining Current Housing Arrangements

Your parents' home, once their castle, can become their prison. It simply can become too much to handle both financially and physically. Unfortunately, the older your parents become, the more resistant they are likely to become to moving away from their familiar environment.

By discussing the possible options available to your parents years before they need to make a decision, you will have an easier time to follow through with alternative housing for them if the need arises. Beside the obvious nursing home option, other options include home sharing, accessory apartments, home care, and continuing care communities.

Inability to Receive Appropriate Health Care

Your parents' real health care problem is the ability to get quality care. Medicare and Medicare Gap insurance are critical. Unfortunately, they are wrapped in bureaucratic *red tape*. And, with the impending health reform, dealing with national insurance will probably become even more cumbersome. You may need to intervene to assist your parents with the *red tape*, inconvenience, and substandard care that may plague them.

In addition, discuss the importance for them to plan financially for their later years. They could begin dollar-cost-averaging into a diversified no-load mutual fund which is earmarked for some of their future health needs. Along with proper insurance, this could go a long way to ensuring adequate funds to cover health care needs. (Consider the top performing funds over the last five-year period in the fund categories of growth, growth and income, or balanced. See Step 16 for specific names.)

The assistance of a fee-for-service Certified Financial Planner could be very valuable in making the proper choices.

Too Little or Too Much Insurance Coverage

While too little insurance can be financially disastrous, too much can simply become an unnecessary expense. The elderly are easy targets for aggressive insurance salespeople who will sell them duplicate or unessential coverage. It is critical to make sure your parents are adequately insured and they purchase or pay no more than they need. Help your parents shop around for the best policies. If they can self-insure to some extent by purchasing no-load mutual funds at an early age with the same dollars which might otherwise go toward a questionable health policy, they may be far better off in the long run.

Lack of Attention to Day-to-Day Financial Matters

If your parents are having difficulty in carrying out their daily financial tasks, you or a financial professional may need to manage their finances. Warning signs include overdue bills, threatened utility cut-offs, and failure to file income tax returns. A *durable power of attorney* and a *living trust* can be beneficial in these situations.

Susceptibility to Dishonest Schemes

Your parents are vulnerable. They are the prey of unscrupulous *scam* artists. From apparently simple home maintenance to expensive personal purchases, there are those who will take advantage of an elderly person's fear and helplessness. To assist your parents from being bamboozled by slick salespeople, you should arrange with them to always consult you whenever they are planning to spend over $500—no matter what. Almost nothing that is worthwhile will ever have to be purchased immediately. There is usually time to think things over first.

Change in Money Habits

If you become aware that your parents are becoming unusually frugal, it could be a sign that they are having financial problems. Many retired people outlive their financial resources, and that fear could lead them to take drastic and unwarranted action. Help them by paying for a financial professional to review their assets and investment plan to be sure your parents are on track with their future financial needs.

Getting involved with your parents' future needs will not only make your parents happy, it will also set an excellent example for your own children for the time when you may need their help. There are also community-based programs available to assist senior citizens. You or your parents could contact the National Association of Area Agencies on Aging by calling 202-296-8130 to obtain detailed information.

21

Enjoy the Harvest of Your Efforts

You will learn . . .

• *four income options available to you at retirement*
• *how to prepare a Withdrawal Table*
• *a method to retire before age 59½ without IRS penalties*

Are you ready? This is the harvest of all your efforts. This is the point where you have reached your goal of financial independence. You are now ready to reap the benefits of your investment portfolio.

Once you've reached this ultimate goal, you have several options to consider. My recommendation is Option #1: Stay with your present plan. Other options include: Relinquish management of the plan; Purchase an immediate, fixed annuity; Purchase zero coupon bonds.

Option #1: Stay With the Plan

Do you want to continue with the investment plan you have been following up to this point? My suggestion is for you to continue. The plan that I have deliberately laid out is a plan that can continue for a lifetime. It *is* a Lifetime Investment Plan. Your only change at this stage will be to begin withdrawing money regularly rather than dollar-cost-averaging into it as you have been. Here's how to make the change.

In Step 17, you learned how to prepare an Annual Monitor table. That table projected what your financial target should be at the end of each year into the future until reaching your goal. It helped you to stay on track. A Withdrawal table is a similar type of table, but in reverse.

A Withdrawal Table (see Figure 21-1) projects how much will be left in your nest egg account at the end of each successive year into the future after: 1. you have taken out your annual living needs at the beginning of the year, and 2. the balance of the portfolio has continued to grow from its investments. Each year your annual withdrawal is projected based on your original needs that you calculated in Step 15 and is increased annually by the projected inflation rate. The annual increase in your withdrawal offsets the decrease in purchasing power as a result of inflation. The bottom line is that your standard of living can be maintained even though inflation continues to increase your cost of living.

I'm going to describe the components of the Withdrawal Table first. Then, I'll return to our young couple, Jodi and Mike, and go through their projected Withdrawal table.

Beginning Balance: This is the value of your nest egg at the beginning of your retirement. It is the *PV* button on the financial calculator.

Years to Withdraw: This is the projected number of years before your portfolio is depleted to nothing. Most financial planners suggest you use your projected life expectancy (see Table 21-1) and then add another ten to fifteen years. It is the N button on the financial calculator. If you prefer not to touch the principal at all, you could enter 1,000 for N which represents infinity for all intents and purposes.

Anticipated annually-compounded rate of return: There is no guarantee you will achieve this return. It is based on the historical returns of the funds you choose. It is always wise to underestimate this number. This is the I button on the financial calculator.

Projected inflation rate: This is what you project to be the annual inflation rate. This is also the percent by which you will increase your annual withdrawals in order to keep up with inflation.

Annual needs in today's dollars: This is what you expect to spend annually in today's dollars to live the lifestyle you desire at retirement.

Figure 21-1: Withdrawal Table

Date _____

Beginning Balance _____
Years to Withdraw _____
Anticipated annually-compounded rate of return _____
Projected inflation rate _____
Annual needs - today's $ _____
Annual needs - future $ _____

Start Yr	Year	Age	Annual	Target	Actual	Adjust
1						
2						
3						
4						
5						

6	7	8	9	10	11	12	13	14	15	16	17	18	19	20	

Figure 21-1: Withdrawal Table (*continued*)

Start Yr	Year	Age	Annual	Target	Actual	Adjust
21						
22						
23						
24						
25						
26						
27						
28						
29						
30						
31						
32						
33						

34	35	36	37	38	39	40	41	42	43	44	45	46	47	48

Table 21-1: Life Expectancy Table

MALE	AGE FEMALE	LIFE EXPECTANCY ADDITIONAL YEARS	MALE	AGE FEMALE	LIFE EXPECTANCY ADDITIONAL YEARS
50	55	25.5	80	85	7.5
51	56	24.7	81	86	7.1
52	57	24.0	82	87	6.7
53	58	23.2	83	88	6.3
54	59	22.4	84	89	6.0
55	60	21.7	85	90	5.7
56	61	21.0	86	91	5.4
57	62	20.3	87	92	5.1
58	63	19.6	88	93	4.8
59	64	18.9	89	94	4.5
60	65	18.2	90	95	4.2
61	66	17.5	91	96	4.0
62	67	16.9	92	97	3.7

63	68	16.2	93	98	3.5
64	69	15.6	94	99	3.3
65	70	15.0	95	100	3.1
66	71	14.4	96	101	2.9
67	72	13.8	97	102	2.7
68	73	13.2	98	103	2.5
69	74	12.6	99	104	2.3
70	75	12.1	100	105	2.1
71	76	11.6	101	106	1.9
72	77	11.0	102	107	1.7
73	78	10.5	103	108	1.5
74	79	10.1	104	109	1.3
75	80	9.6	105	110	1.2
76	81	9.1	106	111	1.0
77	82	8.7	107	112	0.8
78	83	8.3	108	113	0.7
79	84	7.8	109	114	0.6

Annual needs in future dollars: Using a financial calculator, your annual needs are projected into the future taking into consideration the extra amount of money you will need to offset the decrease in purchasing power of the dollar as a result of inflation. (See Step 14 to review the ravages of inflation on your purchasing power and Step 15 to review the concept of future value and the financial calculator.)

Start Year: Year "1" is the first year that you will withdraw an annual income. In this example, you withdraw an annual income at the beginning of the year, place it in a check-writing money market account, and write yourself a check monthly for your needs.

Year: The actual year you begin your withdrawal program.

Age: This is your attained age during that Year.

Annual: Your projected annual need which increases each year by the projected inflation rate. This is the total that you withdraw at the beginning of the year to meet your needs. (All interest earned in the check-writing money market account is a bonus and is not considered in these calculations.)

Target: The projected balance of your nest egg at the end of each Year 1. after you have withdrawn the annual amount at the beginning of the year to be used over the course of the year and 2. after the remainder of the portfolio has grown from its mutual fund investments for that Year.

Actual: The real time balance of your portfolio at the end of the year. You will record this annually as you monitor your Withdrawal table.

Adjust: If the Target balance is less than the Actual balance, you are in good shape. No adjustment is necessary. If, on the other hand, your Target balance is more than the Actual balance, you are running a deficit. Your options at that moment are:

• Shift your mutual funds to better performing funds. (See Step 16.)
• Withdraw less money in the following year.
• Consider some means of supplementing your income aside from your nest egg account.

Now, let's again interrupt Jodi and Mike to discover how they have put their Withdrawal Table together (see Figure 21-2). I think they are cruising somewhere in the Caribbean.

Jodi and Mike's Annual Monitor table has projected their combined nest egg to be worth $1,011,767. They will be 56 years old when they begin retirement at the beginning of 2021. From the Life Expectancy table, they find their combined life expectancy is approximately 25 more years. To be on the safe side, they add 15 years to this and plan their withdrawals for the next 40 years.

Figure 21-2: Withdrawal Table for Jodi and Mike

Date _____

Beginning Balance	$1,011,767	
Years to withdraw	40	
Anticipated annually-compounded rate of return		15%
Projected inflation rate	4.5%	
Annual needs - today's $	$94,057	
Annual needs - future $		

Start Yr	Year	Age	Annual	Target	Actual	Adjust
1	2021		$94,057	$1,055,367		
2	2022		$98,290	$1,100,638		
3	2023		$102,713	$1,147,614		
4	2024		$107,335	$1,196,321		
5	2025		$112,165	$1,246,778		

6	2026		$117,212	$1,299,001
7	2027		$122,487	$1,352,991
8	2028		$127,999	$1,408,741
9	2029		$133,759	$1,466,229
10	2030		$139,778	$1,525,419
11	2031		$146,068	$1,586,253
12	2032		$152,641	$1,648,654
13	2033		$159,510	$1,712,516
14	2034		$166,687	$1,777,703
15	2035		$174,188	$1,844,042
16	2036		$182,027	$1,911,318
17	2037		$192,218	$1,976,965
18	2038		$198,778	$2,044,915
19	2039		$207,723	$2,112,770
20	2040		$217,070	$2,180,055

Figure 21-2: Withdrawal Table for Jodi and Mike (*continued*)

Start Yr	Year	Age	Annual	Target	Actual	Adjust
21	2041		$226,839	$2,246,199		
22	2042		$237,046	$2,310,526		
23	2043		$247,713	$2,372,235		
24	2044		$258,861	$2,430,380		
25	2045		$270,509	$2,483,851		
26	2046		$282,682	$2,531,345		
27	2047		$295,403	$2,571,333		
28	2048		$308,696	$2,602,032		
29	2049		$322,587	$2,621,362		
30	2050		$337,104	$2,626,897		
31	2051		$352,273	$2,615,817		
32	2052		$368,126	$2,584,845		
33	2053		$384,691	$2,530,177		

				$402,002	$2,447,401
34	2054			$402,002	$2,447,401
35	5055			$420,093	$2,331,405
36	2056			$438,997	$2,176,269
37	2057			$458,752	$1,975,145
38	2058			$479,395	$1,720,112
39	2059			$500,969	$1,402,014
40	2060			$523,512	$1,010,278
41	2061			$547,070	$532,689
42					
43					
44					
45					
46					
47					
48					

Using their financial calculator, they determine how much they should withdraw their first year of retirement so that their nest egg will last 40 years.

Here are the calculation entries: N is 40; PV is 1,011,767; I is 10 (anticipated portfolio rate of return adjusted for inflation—see Step 15); FV is 0 (account will be depleted at the end of 40 years). Press the PMT key (the calculator is set for "Begin" payment mode since withdrawals come out at the beginning of each year). The answer is -94,057. (Remember, it is a negative number because you are taking it out of your account.) This is how much Jodi and Mike will take as income their first year of retirement. Each successive year, Jodi and Mike will withdraw 4.5% more to offset the inflation rate of 4.5%.

These of course are only educated guesses just as are all of your projections will be. You will have to reevaluate your calculations and projections annually to be sure things are on target.

Continuing with the Withdrawal table, the annual amounts to withdraw each successive year are increased by the inflation rate. Year "2" equals Year "1" plus 4.5%. Year "3" equals Year "2" plus 4.5%. And so on.

To calculate the Target values, a simple degree of math is required:

1. Begin with the beginning balance *($1,011,767 in Jodi and Mike's case)*;

2. Subtract out the first year's annual needs *($1,011,767 - $94,057 = $917,710)*;

3. To this balance, add in the expected total return for the year *($917,710 + [0.15 times $917,710] = $1,055,367)*.

4. This is the *Target* value at the end of that *Year*.

5. Continue down the table until all *Target* values have been determined.

Jodi and Mike will complete this Withdrawal Table through the last year of their projection which is 40 years from when they retire. It is not until the year 2060 (15 years beyond their combined life expectancy) that their nest egg is close to being depleted.

Option #2: Relinquish Management of the Plan

If you no longer want to deal with the management of your portfolio, you could hire someone else to do it for you. However, you lose control of your money. You could, of course, teach someone to follow your plan to the letter. Remember, no one cares more about your money than you!

Option #3: Purchase Zero Coupon Bonds

You could become much more conservative and decide to liquidate your portfolio and then purchase zero coupon bonds that come due at various dates in the future. Then you could use the proceeds from these bonds as they come due for your source of income for that year. For example, you could purchase a different zero coupon bond coming due each year for the next ten years. Each one's face value would be for the projected amount of money you projected you needed for each of the next ten years. The remainder of your portfolio balance could stay invested in stock funds until you are ready to purchase another batch of zero coupon bonds spaced to come due each successive year for another 10 years, and so on.

Zero coupon bonds are bought at a deep discount to their face value. No interest is received until the maturity date.

Option #4: Purchase an Immediate Fixed Annuity

An *immediate fixed annuity* is a contract you purchase from an insurance company which pays a specific amount to you regularly and which starts right away. You could purchase an *immediate fixed annuity* and begin to have regular payments made to you and your spouse for the remainder of your lives. You will no longer have any need to invest into your retirement account. It will go to purchase the annuity. Be sure there is some type of cost-of-living provision included in the annuity payment schedule so your standard of living can keep up with inflation.

Be aware that a fixed annuity will be based on a much lower rate of return than you would probably earn on your stock mutual fund portfolio. This translates to lower regular payments to you than you projected in Step 15 when you used your stock mutual funds. (To compensate for this reduced return, project a lower inflation-adjusted-rate-of-return on the How Much Does It Take worksheet.)

Retire Before Age 59½

One last note: You do not have to wait until 59½ to retire. Here is an extra piece of information that may influence your decision when to retire. The IRS imposes a penalty if you take money out of your IRA or other tax-deferred retirement program prior to age 59½. On the surface, this may appear to be an effort by the government to collect another tax by enforcing this early withdrawal penalty. But, the real reason is that the government is trying to prevent the undisciplined individual from invading his or her nest egg which has been set aside for retirement.

Depleting a retirement account prematurely could leave an individual with a significant deficit later in retirement. It's not just the amount withdrawn that is lost; it's also the compounded wealth which would otherwise have accumulated from that early withdrawal that is lost.

Here's what happens if you take an early withdrawal:

1. You must pay income taxes on the amount withdrawn, and

2. you must pay a 10% penalty on the amount withdrawn.

Let's get nosey one last time with Jodi and Mike:
Assume they are earning 15% compounded a year on their IRAs, their combined federal and state income tax marginal bracket is now 28%, and they have 5 more years before they reach age 59½. If they withdrew $40,000, they would pay $11,200 in federal and state income taxes and $4,000 in early withdrawal penalties. In other words, 38% of what they took out would have to be paid in taxes.

Another big loss comes from not compounding. That $40,000 would have earned an additional $40,454 if allowed to compound over the following 5 years until they reached age 59½.

However, if you are ready to retire, there is a

way to begin a withdrawal program without paying the 10% penalty. The IRS allows penalty-free withdrawals if *all* of the following conditions are met:

• You must receive substantially equal payments based on your life expectancy;
• You must receive these payments at least once a year for a minimum of 5 years; and
• You must receive these payments beyond age 59½.

Jodi and Mike have decided to retire when they reach 56 years of age. Since they will meet the requirements I have just outlined, they will not have to pay any IRS penalties.

So, if you have accumulated enough money in your tax-deferred plan, and you are ready to retire before age 59½, you may be able to do so without penalty. The key is to receive annual payments for at least 5 years without stopping payments until you are at least past the age of 59½. This can begin at any age before age 59½. You or your accountant can do some simple computations to determine the amount you must withdraw annually to meet the above requirement based on your life expectancy.

To get more information, speak to your tax advisor to crunch the numbers to see what works best for you. You should also call the IRS at 800-

829-3676 and request Publication 575 (Pension and Annuity Income) and Publication 939 (Pension General Rule). These publications are very detailed but very informative. They are also free.

You've purchased my book to learn my philosophy. And, you have learned it. Good luck! Reaching financial security is not as difficult as many investment salespeople would have you believe. But, it does take work and commitment.

The last half-piece of this puzzle is the finishing touch. It is the final motivation to get you off your indecision pad. It's what makes the frog finally jump!

Go for it!

21½

The Final ½ Step

So, what makes up a "half of a step?" It's not necessarily half the length of an average step, and it's certainly not half as informative. It is, however, different.

Here, I have assembled a series of bullet (•) points. These are points of importance and reference. I have pulled them from the first 21 steps of the book and present them here for your easy access:

- Get organized!
- Get serious!
- Get started!
- Update your Personal Financial Statement at least annually. Keep past statements as a history of your financial growth.
- Update your Cash Flow Statement at least annually. Retain these past statements to document your spending habits.
- Write down your goals. The most successful people are those who have written goals.
- Identify your needs. Remember, live beneath your means.

- Set up an emergency account in a money market fund that contains between three and six months' living expenses. This is your "security blanket."
- Purchase insurance only for catastrophic losses—losses which you cannot afford to assume personally.
- Compounding is the "eighth wonder of the world." It makes your wealth accumulation plan work for you. Use it!
- Debt is more expensive than you think. It can stop you dead in your tracks from reaching your financial goals.
- Be sure you are buying a home for the right reasons. Renting may be financially more advantageous over the long-term.
- Know what you can do to avoid taxes legally. Know what you can do to defer taxes. Take advantage of the tax laws; they have been given to you as a gift by the United States Congress.
- Be sure to prepare a will, a living will, and a durable power of attorney.
- Several trusts can assist you in your journey to financial security. Several to consider are: a revocable trust, a credit trust, a 2503(c) trust, and a charitable remainder trust.
- No-load mutual funds are excellent ways to participate in the growth potential of the stock markets in the U.S. and around the world.

- The Value Ratio is a well documented method of identifying when the U.S. stock market is severely overvalued or severely undervalued.
- Everyone has a specific temperament when investing for various financial goals. Make sure you know your *Investment Temperature* before you begin investing. If you don't, you could be asking for trouble.
- Only invest in those categories of funds which fit your Investment Temperature.
- Risk is smoothed out as your time horizon increases.
- Inflation is an insidious tax that erodes the purchasing power of your hard-earned money. All of your investments must take this into consideration.
- Learn to use a financial calculator. It will assist you with many calculations for future planning.
- Use your Personal Financial Statement and Cash Flow Statement to project your needs for retirement into the future.
- Choose the best no-load mutual funds over the past 5 year period.
- There are over 30 no-load mutual funds that have average compounded annual returns of 15% or greater over the last 10 year period.
- Discount brokers offer a simple way to invest in several no-load mutual funds. Only one phone

call is required to transact all of your business, and record keeping is simplified through one monthly statement.

- Dollar-cost-average!
- Monitor, monitor, monitor!
- Make adjustments as necessary along the way. No plan is fool-proof. No plan is guaranteed. No plan takes No effort.
- Help your parents cope with future life changes before these changes become crises in their lives and in yours.
- Take pride in the fact that you have accomplished what you have set out to do.
- Enjoy the harvest of your efforts. You have earned it. You are in the unique position to live the lifestyle you and your spouse have chosen for the remainder of your glorious lives.

Important Contacts

- Major discount brokers: See Step 16, pages 148-149.
- The best no-load mutual funds of each fund category. See Step 16, pages 142-143.
- Over 30 funds with 15% or greater total returns over the past 10 years: See Step 16, pages 144-145.
- Answers to your insurance questions: National Insurance Consumer Help Line (800-942-4242).

- Fee-for-service term life insurance search: Insurance Information Inc. (800-472-5800)

- Insurance company rating resources, available in most libraries: A. M. Best & Co (800-424-2378); Moody's Investors Services (212-553-0377); and Standard & Poors Insurance Rating Services (212-208-1527).

- Fee-for-service insurance company information: Weiss Research (800-289-9222).

- Credit reporting companies: TRW (800-392-1122), Trans Union (800-851-2674), Equifax (800-685-1111).

- Variable annuity search: Independent Advantage Financial and Insurance Services, Inc. (800-829-2887).

- Free IRS publications (800-829-3676)

- Getting organized for estate planning: *The Beneficiary Book* (800-222-9125).

- Information regarding wills and trusts: Wealth Transfer Planning, Inc., (Charles Douglas, JD, CFP or Cory Grant, JD 800-423-4890).

- No-load mutual fund information sources: *The Individual Investor's Guide to Low-Load Mutual Funds*, *Mutual Fund Quarterly Update* (312-280-0170); *Morningstar No-Load Funds* (800-876-5005).

- Department of Social Security (800-772-1213)

- *Young Investor Parent's Guide* by Liberty Financial Company, (800-338-2550).

• Information on resources for the elderly: National Association of Area Agencies on Aging (202-296-8130).

• Dr. Danenberg's newsletter on mutual fund investing for a lifetime: *Market Focus* (800-825-7850).

How long did it take for you to read this book? Next time, it will take less. And, the time after that, even less. You see, you will want to reread this book several times. Each time you reread it, you will pick up another pearl, and then another, and still another. Keep this book within easy reach as a handy reference and motivator.